The World In Between

From the Collection of Robert Milkwood Thomas

The World In Between

◆

A Walk for Unknown Lands

Robert Sungmanitu
Tanka Wayawawicakiya

Writers Club Press
San Jose New York Lincoln Shanghai

The World In Between
A Walk for Unknown Lands

Writers Club Press
an imprint of iUniverse, Inc.

For information address:
iUniverse, Inc.
5220 S. 16th St., Suite 200
Lincoln, NE 68512
www.iuniverse.com

ISBN: 0-595-21019-8

Printed in the United States of America

Dedication

◆

First, this book is being dedicated to my father, Samuel Melodia. He knew from when I was young that something else was there but kept it to himself until later on in my life. We had many talks of things that I was learning. There were many things he learned in reverse. It was a two way street. He did many things for me that I will always be grateful for.

There was a lot of learning going on and he managed to keep a lot of things together at the same time. He was well liked by many and was no doubt despised by a few, as with all people. He helped me learn what I know today. There were many things that he knew about but was unable to completely fill in due to his passing over.

In many of our talks, we shared many personal things that brought us even closer. He knew what was going on around him but many times refused to speak. His actions spoke many things in many ways. I will always be grateful for all the things he taught me, down to fixing the many parts of a car. Many things both internal and external I will remember and will pass on to my children. In this way his legacy and teachings will continue on.

Secondly, I dedicate this book to my grandfather, Charles Running River. One who was outside of the family but was every bit of it. He taught me all the things my father could not. He was full-blooded Lakotah but was raised in the Dakotah ways of the Teton Council Fire. I visited my grandfather for many years, up until he decided to walk his path to the Spirit World.

He knew many of the things I now know today. He taught a lot of the ceremonies, many of them were very personal. He was a man I strongly looked up to. He refused to be a part of anything that would tear the People apart. He refused the tribal role in the early years because the government murdered his family. He felt the role was another way to control the People. He was not a "hang around the fort Indian" as they were called. He was very independent and stayed on his own no matter what his financial means were.

I was disappointed that he did not have children to follow in his path but this was his decision. I honored him for it rather than feel sorry. He walked his own path his way, no one else's.

Thirdly, I dedicate this book to my children Jennifer, Andrew, Edward, Ashley and Jonathan whom I will pass on this knowledge and much more. They will know what I have learned and I hope they will carry it through to their children. This book will act like a guide for them when things don't always seem or feel right.

The children are our future and must be nurtured. They will pass on our knowledge and wisdom to their children and their children's children so that they will know the ways. The Knowledge must carry on so that the People move forward.

Last but not least, I wish to thank both Sally and to Amey for their part in bearing these children. It is not an easy task to bear children. Many men take advantage of or ignore this. The women take on their roles many times without thought to themselves and many times receive little recognition for it. To the gender of women I honor your efforts and abilities. Without these the role of mother could never be filled.

Robert Sungmanitu Tanka Wayawawicakiya

Tribute to a Mother, a Comrade and a Dear Friend

A woman I greatly respected walked onto her path to the Spirit World. She is riding on the wings of an Eagle to her place among the Ancestors. To her I will say many prayers on the smoke of my pipe onto the Wind to the Great Spirit.

We had many conversations that enlightened both of us to the many aspects of things occurring around us. Her wit made me laugh many times. Her way of "seeing" allowed things to run a little smoother.

We had many talks that paved the way for many things to occur in her life as well as my own. I will honor the words she spoke and hope that they will continue on in other's lives she has touched.

I will pray to the Creator so that her spirit will ride forever free. Her spirit will no longer be burdened by physical constraints. I will prepare a ceremony for her before she rides her last ride to the West.

Your spirit rides free of any pain that you have suffered through this life. It is my hope that others will follow your spirit as you have followed your heart and did what you wanted to do.

Until we meet again, I will honor your spirit for you have shown your heart no matter where you were. May your children listen to your words for these words have spoken softly within their ears.

I hope many will listen to your words long after you are gone from this world. To your spirit I pay tribute to, honor to and ride with you as you make your ride to your family that awaits you.

To you Raven Wolf I pay tribute to this day and remember you 'till we meet again.

Ride strong Kola for I will be standing proud on this mountain watching you go by. I will dress for you so that you will see me as I am.

For you Raven Wolf I stand proud and strong.

Sungmanitu Tanka

Epigraph

───────◆───────

When you stop walking you stop living.

When you stop living, your spirit ceases to learn.

When your spirit ceases to learn, you no longer know who you are.

Contents

Forward ....*xv*

Preface ....*xvii*

Introduction ....*xix*

Are You Religious or Are You Spiritual? *1*

What You Think You See You Don't *4*

The View No One Wants to See *6*

Animals *9*

Native Americans and The New Age Mumbo Jumbo *11*

Diversions *14*

Justice and Law *16*

Beliefs *18*

Journey to the Past *20*

Living A Lie *22*

Freedom *24*

Enrollment *26*

Musical Response *28*

The Tiniest of Them All *30*

The Puddle and The Lake *32*

Balance *34*

Old Ways of the Ancestors *36*

The Wind and the Cetan (Hawk) *38*

The Deer and the Gifts They Leave *40*

The River *42*

Mother Earth *45*

In That Moment *47*

Walking the Red Road *50*

Journey on the Edge of a Storm *52*

Journey Across the Divide *58*

Weather *60*

The Heart of the Land 64

The Bridge 67

Ego vs. Pride 69

Guardians of the Land 70

White Road 74

Why There Are Trees 76

Between Sight and Sound 79

What is "Medicine?" 80

Respect 82

The Coyote Walks Among Us 85

Within The Calm of the Wind 87

The Path of the Spirits, The Path of the Past 89

The Unspoken Words 91

Walk Among The Oaks 93

The Limit of Infinity 96

The Path of the Future Lies in the Past 99

Decision Making 102

The Fire 105

Within the Change of the Seasons 109

Journeys Within the Change of Seasons 111

Is It Imagination or Is It Real 113

On the Side of that Road 116

Path to Advancement or Road to Destruction? 119

Walking in Forgotten Lands 122

The "Feel" of It 125

A Walk Into Gentleness 128

A Walk Into Change 132

The Native Trail of Knowledge 138

As Mother Earth Opens Her Heart 143

The Tree And The Flower 145

Knowing Where The Path Walks 147

Walking with Courage takes Endurance 149

Walking the Road Back 151

Within Life 154

Walking in the Lands of Another 156

The Dilemma of Animals and Their Trust 159

Walking Within The Sacred Circle 161

Walking an Unknown Road into Tomorrow *165*
Where Does Strength Lie? *169*
A Slow Journey *171*
Road of the Dead *173*
Walking a Road into the Past *175*
Knowing Where The Path Walks *177*
Lacking Assimilation *179*
Winged Ones *181*
As the Sun Walks *183*
Another's Walk into Desperation *185*
In Time *187*
Sungmanitu Tanka (The Wolf) *190*

Forward

◆

Whenever anyone speaks it comes around in whatever way the Great Spirit makes his way.

I speak to people as I do anywhere or anytime. Speaking up front to people is the only way. They then know where you stand at all times. People will respect you better for this.

Your voice may become very emotional and speak volumes of your willingness to bring a perspective to light.

Truth comes in its own time and not out like gasoline on a fire. This causes many innocent people to get burned who were never involved. You have to look around and see who is around you and ask if you are willing to take the responsibility of fixing things that are burned from your words.

Who is right or wrong is not the question.

It seems to be a ploy with people that they seek satisfaction of displaying or parading things in front of people for their own ego satisfaction.

This is not a good way.

Now I may be thick here in some way.

But tell me, why keep the clouds and smoke stirring when they really want to clear out?

Preface

◆

The World in Between
By
Robert Sungmanitu Tanka Wayawawicakiya

This book is being written due to the possible lack of understanding of how people try to view the world around them. Many view it with misunderstanding. This book is for people who do not understand what Nature and our place in it truly means. This book also tells of things of the heart. A road not easily followed. I hope this will be a bridge that will help people better understand the connection of not only Nature but the heart itself. This is a glimpse of how I view my world as I grew up in two worlds. These pages are my views on what I have seen and see right now.

Who I am is who I am. Not a mixture of things that have no recorded value, or to someone for the purposes of getting something. This will stand for itself and how I viewed and still view my world. What I have experienced in life stands for itself as truth for me. It stands for what I have learned and been taught.

The current wave of "Native Americanism" is both a blessing and a travesty in itself. This continual exploitation of the People and their practices for the pleasure of those that pay to be "Native American" for a day has to stop. These people will stick around for as long they desire until the "convenience" wears off or they tire of it. It is good for it finally opens the book of truth on what "really" has happened to my brothers and sisters.

This is the story of but one view of the world around me. A view of the society that I both live within and without. My apologies to those that would seem offended, as this is not my intention. Sometimes words from another point of view open up wounds we would rather not see. We create our own blindness as we move along on our path. The words Native Americans, Indians and First Nations are being used interchangeably even though they are "**not**" the same in meaning.

Pilamayayelo.
Sungmanitu Tanka

Introduction

◆

Within these pages are words that you may or may not like. You may not want to listen to what is spoken here. These words speak of things that have happened and of things to come. There are markers to look for and listen to.

There are words spoken about many things. Some good, some not so good to hear. You must decide if what you are reading has some value to things spoken and seen.

There may be disagreements on things. Many things are seen around the fire. Many words spoken. Many ways seen. This will make the fire burn stronger.

Come and sit by the fire and we will tell our stories. Enjoy good food. Enjoy each other's company. We will listen to what is and what will be. We will open our hearts and minds to things spoken, seen and felt. We will hear and see other ways present and walk the Circle together.

The fire will burn strong and warm us.

Come sit.

We will see what we can make for our children.

Are You Religious
or Are You Spiritual?

◆

When I was growing up, I went to church like most people. I did the usual routine asked and then went home. I have always wondered about this. I would sit there in church not knowing exactly what I was doing. I just decided to go with the flow as I was told by my parents. My dad always had different ideas regarding these rituals. He thought it was a waste of time because when people got outside the doors they went back to the same people they were. There was no change in them. Not what appeared to be "forgiveness" on their part. This concept was not a true concept because it was better to tolerate and allow them to learn. There was no true word for this in the language of the People.

I remember one day walking outside the doors to the parking lot and out came this shout "Get the hell out of my way you stupid idiot." He just said, "Ignore them." This person that shouted this was a "pillar" of our church…an elder. After that day I looked at the "church" in a different light than I ever had before.

As I went to Sunday school I started to ask questions that the teacher at times would not like. I asked questions about who Jesus "really" was and what he stood for. As usual I would get the words out of the Bible. They would never tell me "who" he was. Reading it out of a book did nothing for me. I wanted to know "who and what" he "really" was. They would become defensive to my inquiries. The "teachers" never answered them "straight." I would learn that very few who "knew" who he was.

Following a religion doesn't mean you are spiritual and visa versa. I am not knocking religions in any way, quite the contrary. I would like to see people become more attached to the Great Spirit whatever path they follow. A trait that should be practiced more often is to learn to understand the ability of someone to follow their path to the Creator and not mix a bunch of other paths. Mixing of paths doesn't work for anyone no matter what you do. It is like a mountain lion following the ways of a rabbit. You cannot be someone else—only yourself.

So why try to do something that your not able to do? Trying is one thing, taking a path and placing it on your own path and mixing them can't work.

Religion is one path. Spirituality is another. Religions mix these two together. They are not able to keep their people within their structures built for this purpose. The fulfillment these people are trying to find, they can't. The spirit longs for something much deeper and closer to the Great Spirit that does not cause a division between themselves and the Great Spirit. W hen there is division between them then the voice of the Great Spirit becomes lost and the spirit cannot hear it.

The Great Spirit never meant for us to be separated from him by intermediaries. It is strictly a one on one sort of thing that must be maintained so that the Great Spirit can speak to that spirit alone. Nothing between them.

What is right for you may not be right for someone else. This is why there is so much chaos within this world and on Turtle Island. People are not allowed to walk their own path the way that is best for them. There has to be a set mold everyone wants to put everything in. It doesn't work. We are all different even though we are all made from the Great Spirit. Every path is different and has a different sort of circumstances. They have to learn to live through it in order to fulfill what they must learn.

I can no more tell someone else what to do as that person can to me. Once you tell someone something and they follow it you are responsible for that person's problems until such time the Great Spirit removes that responsibility. It can be a hard lesson for you to learn.

The key to what you want is to remain open to the Great Sprit for answers and listening closely to what he is speaking. He knows how to take care of you better than you do. So why not listen? The choice is up to you. No one can tell you otherwise.

What You Think You See You Don't

———————————————— ◆ ————————————————

Much of what is seen is seen with prejudiced or "colored" eyes. We do not see them as they really are regardless of what it may be. We carry so many things with us that help to twist our perception in some way of what we see. Grandfather always taught, "What you think you see you do not." It took quite a number of years before I started to see what he was saying. We color our perceptions of what we see by our experiences and what teachings we learned. Is there a stream sparkling in the sunlight or is your eyesight blinded to other things present there. There were many stories that crossed his lips. Here is one that I remember quite well.

Once there was a wicasa wakan that had to choose who was going to be his successor. The ones he felt he could trust with the knowledge, he narrowed down to two. It took some time to narrow this down because not just anyone could fulfill his role. He had not married so there were no children to take up his position and tasks. He had to choose from the ones he knew had an interest. They must be trustworthy with the knowledge he would give them. It took a special person to fill this because the commitment it would take was not an easy one. They would have to very young and learn, as they grew older. They would need to grow into their skill and wisdom just as he did.

Never to impart the knowledge of the Plant Nations, the Stone Nations, or any other knowledge that was sacred. "One test only will it take for me to choose." The two boys were present with the permission of their parents. He walked them down the path to a stream. There he asked them what they saw in that stream as it flowed by. The first boy said, "I see rocks at the bottom, fish swimming all around, frogs jumping near the waters edge with plants growing nearby, some in and some out. He then asked the second boy what he saw. The boy replied, "I see the sun sparkling along the surface. It shines like a brightly polished stone. I see different kinds of waves flowing in many ways but all in the same direction. But I do not see what lies beneath it even though my eyes see what is in front of me." The wicasa wakan just smiled. He knew who his next apprentice would be.

This boy had the vision for today but also what was more important was that he had the vision for the future. He will see that our people will remain safe for many moons and many seasons to come. He cannot only see on the surface but he has the potential of seeing what is inside. There are things that are not as they appear sometimes. You just look to the heart of it to see what the true meaning is. It just will not come up to you and say, "Here I am!" What is around you is not always what it appears to be.

The View No One Wants to See

◆

What I have become I am proud of and would not be anyone else but myself. I have traveled a hard road with many turns and bumps along the way. I have grown in my knowledge of the world around me. How everything interacts together. Grandfather told me, "You are what you believe yourself to be." I have grown in the ways of the Lakotah as Grandfather has taught so patiently. I am proud to be apart of the People even though I am not. Now you think, "I am in a contradiction of words. Either you are or you are not…which one is it?"

Grandfather refused enrollment in the Council Fires of the Lakotah and Dakotah People in South Dakota. He refused to be a part of the government's continual onslaught of trying to screw the People any way that they could. He said he had no family left for they have killed them. So why should I become a part of something that has killed my family. I am not a "hang around the fort" Indian. He spoke of many things throughout our times together.

Many families died as a result of the government interference and ways of doing things. Many used the government for their own prosperity and gain. There still are many who run our Nations who take most of the money and leave little for the rest…. the wasicus of our People. Large tracts of land where taken from the People by ranchers who used the government for their gain. These people tried to justify their large holdings of land that was not rightfully theirs to have. Large ranches of huge square miles dotted the land. This land that was rightly the people of First Nations.

What do you think would happen if I right now went onto another's land and said, "I now own this land. You do not. Get off or the government will throw you off and no enumeration is yours. Tough luck chump!" Now what do you think you would do? Do you actually think you would not fight for what was "supposedly" yours? You would and you know it.

Our people were no different and they fought back against this sort of theft that still occurs today. No, our people are not to blame for what happened. What happened was in self-defense no matter which way you look at it.

The government sent troops to protect these people who had no business being on the land to begin with. They claimed it was theirs when they just plopped their behinds anywhere they felt they deserved to be. The government was really a government of the wasicus and the rich. Just as much now as it was back then. They did the bidding of the rich and companies that wanted to rape the land and the people for anything that they could, as fast as they could. They then left the wasteland behind for our people to live on.

What the government, the history books say, is in fact twisted from the truth in order not to portray our country as evil and self serving. It portrays it as a righteous country with good moral character. If you investigated for yourself what was done to the Native Peoples of this land you would no longer think yourself as a free and righteous person.

This country was founded on the death and destruction of the People of Turtle Island. Not some conquering nation who seems to think it has done something right. This land was never conquered. Treaties were signed. Then the land was stolen. The so-called wonderful days of the past are splattered with death and blood flowing like rivers across this land. It continues to this day at an unending pace.

These were and still are tragic days. Tragic days that the people of this land seem to conveniently forget or refuse to accept responsibility for. They say they are not responsible for what has happened in the past. This is far from the truth. If you walk upon a man killing another man and you ignore them are you responsible for what you knew full well what was happening? Yes you are. Just as guilty as the man who did the killing is. Most of the Native Nations were forced onto reservations…land the government didn't want. Land that they knew was worthless at the time and would causes our people to die. It was either die or be assimilated into the present society.

Grandfather knew how stupid and foolish the leaders were. Not only among the People but also in the dominant society that he lived both within and without. It reminded him of the old story of how the dogs always tried to smell each other's butt to see who smelled better.

You can close your eyes for a while but eventually they will open and what you will see you will not like.

Animals

◆

As I sit here today, finally outside in the sun when it is not so cold, I started to feel again one with the Winged Ones, Four-Leggeds and Mother Earth. I sat gliding with the two Cetans, Hawks, that showed up today after a bit of an absence. I was gliding with them on the wind and feeling the gentle breeze beneath their wings. Feeling better from the weight of many issues going on around me. Feeling their power and gentleness and the feelings they were feeling. One of being close to the Creator, the Wind and Mother Earth…all in unity together.

The Cetan has watched over many trips I have traveled. Flying close by or sitting there watching as I go by. Today was different though because I got a closer glimpse of their wisdom and power. Feeling of being so close to the Wind as it flows through these feathers. I gained a stronger bond of respect from it. A feeling that I am never alone within the Creator's world.

The Four-Leggeds in their wisdom and power will always guide and take care of your needs. The pair of them, the Cetans, flying so free without the worries we have…sometimes the senseless worries. The feeling of gentleness the Wind brings when flowing through, the whisper of its voice, the Wind and the Hawks together. Both are very powerful but yet so gentle. Ever watching and flowing as carefree as they can be.

The Cetan is an important symbol to us because of its ability to see. It sees things that are far beyond our scope to see and hear. The Cetan flies on the wind with such grace and power. Many are afraid of this creature and really have no right to be. They have families and babies like all other families. They fly over large territories and keep an eye on what is happening throughout its land.

The power and grace it shows is an example for us to follow. Its power comes from its strength, a strength that emanates from itself no matter where it stands. Its power and strength originate in the Great Spirit. Cetan is his name in the Lakotah language. It is derived for its endurance and swiftness.

The Great Spirit and the Ancestors watch through their eyes. Ever watching our moves and guiding those that are willing to watch and listen to their teachings. The feeling I felt with them is something I could not ever put to words. That feeling is welcomed anytime with my brother, the Cetan. The respect that is due to them and the wisdom they impart is something that must be felt and experienced.

Native Americans and
The New Age Mumbo Jumbo

◆

The mixing of Native American ways and all this New Age stuff is quite confusing. I have yet to understand why this really is. There is no correlation whatsoever between these two. It seems that many people are trying to mix these two and they do not mix. Never have and never will. They are not even close to each other in any way.

Today there are so many people trying to place symbols of ours into their creations. Claiming that this is their path and they have a right to follow it. How can you claim what is not yours. You then mix it with something that has no connection. I look at all these New Age booths and books and wonder what these people are thinking. Where are they coming from? Where in the world are they going? This seems like almost total blindness to me. Almost like wandering through a mist, fog or smoke without a flashlight.

We as Native Peoples have a spiritual way that is not like any other. We follow our path that is no one else's. We do not follow another's or mix them. I do not know how my brothers and sisters can mix Christianity and Native ways. It seems to be a conflict of interest to me. You are trying to mix two identities into one. This is not our way. There are companies and individuals exploiting our ways and trying to make people "Native American." How could you ever possibly do this? Many have not traveled this road before. It is like trying to run down a rabbit with flippers on your feet. Being "Native" is not like an occupation. It's not "Well I think I will be Native today." It is not a switching of hats whenever one pleases or is in the mood.

The Canku Luta is not a convenience sort of thing. You travel this road for life. There is no turning back once you are on it. You are on it from birth unless in some way your path became hidden. Then someone or something happened that came along and finally snapped you out of your dream world. It made you realize who you "really" were. There are no flights of fancy in our world or on this path—the Canku Luta or Red Road.

It is a hard road to keep for everyone wants to convert to something that they seem to think will change your life. Convert you into something miraculous and life will be better after that. Well, I hate to burst your bubble but it does not work like that. The one thing I do not like is somebody trying to come up to me and convert me for his or her needs, gains or into some religion I do not want to be a part of. If I wanted to be converted I would walk into a church and ask for it.

The ceremonies on this road are not like other ways in this world. You give thanks to all that lives within this world. You are thankful to be a part of it. Thanking the Creator and all the spirits that help you every day. All the creatures of this world that help sustain the life we lead. The Plant Oyates that grow to sustain our being with the sacrifices that they give to our tables. We just give thanks to all things around us that we are a part of…not separate from.

One thing that I have noticed about other people is that they seem to think that they are separate from Mother Earth. They seem to think that they did not come from her womb and grow to be whom they are. If it was not for all of nature itself there would be no one around to enjoy this beauty that we have around us. The Creator created all of this for Mother Earth nurtures and us to health and keeps us that way. In my opinion New Ageism is something like having a constant high and never coming down from it. They have many high ideas with no attachment on the ground.

What needs to happen is they need to get down on their knees and watch the ants to see what they are doing. They need to listen to the Wind and hear what is being whispered there.

Listen to what the animals—your brothers and sisters—have to say about what you are doing. How it is affecting them, listen to their wisdom that they try to speak. When you come to know all that is around you then you might see a slight bit of what it is like to be Native.

Diversions

◆

I do not know about others but I have seen many things that have caused diversions in our life. Things like politics, sickness, emotionally charged issues, intellectualism and the many other things that permeate our existence. Are we as individuals watching our directions carefully enough to allow the small things in life to co-exist within our paths as the larger issues? If the smaller issues sit around to fend for themselves then the bigger issues remain unsettled. The smaller issues never become addressed because the larger issues at hand overshadow them. I look at the small wonders present all over and wonder if anyone verbalizes the small things. It seems people's preoccupation with the larger things always put the smaller ones on the back burner.

Like if the ants within our soils are getting the food necessary to survive within their world. Are we trying to help things around them but end up destroying things with our carelessness and they just have to fend for themselves? We walk all over them. We show little appreciation for what being done by them and their place in this life. How do we know what we are doing is "good" for the whole. Is it our nearsighted vision occurring? Without the small things being solved the bigger things will only get worse. You cannot create fertile ground unless all the parts are working. To create the ground necessary for things to grow you need all the ingredients necessary to maintain healthy growth. If you do not work on each part how is the whole going to survive?

This land cannot last when we are diverted. Our focus must remain within the confines of the life we lead. The Land cannot support us if we are not balancing the Land with our needs. The society you live in may be trying on purpose to divert you from the real issues. There are so many issues we are dealing with in our lives that the bigger picture becomes lost.

We are so concerned with our smaller worlds that we forget about all the other slices of the circle and what it needs to show us. The land, animals, our lives, Plants, Winged Ones and many other things revolve around the same circle. We cannot be constantly diverted to other less important things than the survival of our Lands and People.

The family is important to follow and not to become diverted from. Focusing on one thing at a time and solving each one will help eliminate these diversions we are being slammed with. Like a rock hitting the ground.

If you become too close in your vision take a walk. This will allow it to open up so that you will see other things going on around you. Watch the Winged Ones fly by and talk to their friends and family. Feel the Trees speak their language and show them what they really have to offer besides the wood that they are made of.

Listen to what the Great Spirit is saying through all the creatures that live around you. The Land is a part of you, not separate as we are led to believe through poor teaching. You would be surprised what you will hear and what will speak to you. In time you will become a part of things and they will become a part of you.

Justice and Law

◆

Thinking and struggling with the struggles of my People and of all Peoples around the world is something that takes much energy. I am sitting here at almost 1 am pacing around the house with multitudes of thoughts. I pace struggling with the words "law" and "justice." Two totally different words. Each one at opposite ends of the scale. Can law be justice or justice be law? Can neither one ever meet in a balanced way as the statue of justice so stands?

Laws are made to protect us and balance things so no one takes advantage of another. But if these laws are broken and a price paid, is it justice? Has "justice" been served? As we file lawsuits to get back things taken from us and get laws passed to help us in our struggles are we truly serving "justice?" Or are we serving the law for our people in order to prove justice.

Creating laws is one thing…justice is another depending on the viewpoint you stand from. To what end will justice be served for us? How much "justice" is enough? How many laws are enough to create justice or to serve it? When will the cycle end in this regard? Will the circle keep going round and round until we're exhausted by the weight?

Between all these words, I am trying to figure out a path between all this. A way forward that is a balanced way and still trying to listen to the Great Spirit's words as he points the way. I think it is just my nervousness and at times uncertainty on this path that brings me to this point.

Holding on to what knowledge was taught regarding "justice" and the exercise of it in all situations as best as possible. If I do this or do that will I serve justice in doing so?

Everyone has had a different viewpoint as to what justice should be but never a concrete answer. So…are we serving an image of "justice" or are we serving our own "satisfaction" of what justice should be?

It is not accident that most of the "judges" are lawyers and have little knowledge of common sense. They refuse to step outside the boundaries of "law" and make a different road that would be the right way to follow. There are too many that just think they are doing what is right. All they are doing is perpetuating the continual onslaught of injustice on our People and many others.

Justice can only be served when the "actual" truth is out and in the open. Without this kind of openness and without "all" evidence brought in, justice will "never" be served. I am quite amazed on how the law can be twisted in so many ways to gain "justice" for the one that is looking for it. Many are convicted who are innocent and many others not convicted who are truly guilty.

So, it this justice or is it law?

Beliefs

◆

I must put to words what I hear and feel right now. These words are not shared by all but a few. The belief in the Great Spirit for what it is. Belief varies from person to person and from path to path. No one is the same. No one shares the same experiences as another so the beliefs are different but still yet the same.

Truth "always" stays its path no matter what…it "never" deviates for anyone. To follow the path to the Great Spirit is one that must be followed by and through the heart. Not the mind with all its baggage…but the heart. No organization, place, church, building or anything of any kind can be used to reach the heart. The heart can be covered with things that cloud it and not allow it to see properly be they emotions, events, thoughts, and actions. Anything can cause blindness within the reaches of the heart.

Grandfather always said, "the heart is within the spirit but without the spirit there is no heart". We do our daily things ignoring the many things around us. Never listening to what the heart is telling us. We create things that we hope will show others who and what we are. But it really doesn't matter for it will disappear like dust thrown into the wind. Belief in the Great Spirit has no walls or material goods to represent it…just the "heart" of it.

What we believe is based on our own perceptions of things around us. It is based on how we experienced things in the past. How we grew up. The people who influenced us as we were growing up. Beliefs vary so widely that it is dizzying to watch and see.

Many believe the Spirit World is something that exists outside our realm of "reality." Like the Land we are not a part of. I know it to be very close even though we travel the spirit road to get to it. It is a place that we go to see our families and Ancestors. A place we are proud of. The place where the Great Spirit resides.

Ceremonies help to bring us closer to the Great Spirit. We send our prayers on the smoke of our Pipe onto the Wind and up to the Great Spirit. The world of the unseen can only be seen and experienced with the heart. The mind cannot grasp what it cannot see nor feel. The Great Spirit speaks to the heart and your belief helps to build a bridge for you to walk across. As I do my ceremonies to the Great Spirit I hope that he hears that which I speak to him. And to all the Spirits in the Four Corners and Mother Earth I hold my beliefs and whisper my prayers.

Journey to the Past

◆

As I walked through the grasses of the prairie on the rez I started to feel the images of the past move around my vision. I was starting to walk through the memories of my Ancestors that once walked this Land. The Land took care of them, fed them and gave them all that they needed. I walk watching the movements of my People upon the Land. Walking through the children playing their games. The women doing their beading, cleaning the hides and taking care of the smaller ones.

Walking through the memories of the meetings of the People that were necessary to keep the Tribe on the right path and to talk of things to come and of things that once were. To talk of things that had to be seen and thought about. Walking through the many homes of my People. All made in a different manner but yet the same. Decorated depending on the position of the person and how he/she worked to earn what they had. The honor bestowed upon themselves and/or their families. Others not so elaborate…rather plain in nature but yet speaks just as much as the others.

The wisdom spoken by the wicasa wakans or winyan wakans. The feeling of peace and contentment among the People. The dolls the small girls play with. The teaching of the boys of the things they would need not only for manhood but also for life itself. The teachings and wisdom of the Old Ones set to stories for the young ones to grasp so they understood about themselves and what was expected of them. They were the

Storytellers of the Tribe. A great deal of knowledge spoken from their lips. They taught the history and lessons of the People.

Feeling the Earth beneath my feet that was unpolluted and clean. The air is fresh, clear and crisp. Once again the past will return but not until we learn to be who we really are. Not some fools who seem to think that the techno crap of today will bring us peace, wisdom or feed our children. Solve our problems and show us the way.

The past holds it's gifts if we really want to see what is there. It teaches many things and allows us to learn from the mistakes. It allows us to see the "real" truth and not a distorted viewpoint.

Some say that the past should be left in the past and only build on it as we go. How can we build on something that is little known? Or if it is known and not what we want to see are we going to change it to justify what we really want to see.

Building a secure foundation and not one that will disintegrate in a short time is a necessary goal. Journeying to the past is necessary to learn things not only the mistakes but to learn what was lost. If you look back even at yourself there is much to relearn that has been missed. To not make the same mistakes that are being made today.

Think about it. One day you'll see your answers change.

Living A Lie

◆

Many wonder why things always come around in a circle constantly without ever seemingly ever getting off a particular circle. The circle of how the wasicus are going to deal with the past. It seems this is a rather hard thing to do for many because of what is at stake for most on Turtle Island. I have yet to understand why this is so hard for many to accept.

When something is stolen and you continue to live on land not rightfully yours why is it so hard to accept this? The reason is that you have probably worked hard for what you have and now you feel comfortable with it. Don't want to give up what you have worked hard for. Now.... what if what you worked for is total disillusionment on your part? Part of a false belief that was bred into you from the beginning...much like smoke and mirrors. How do you solve this problem? Kind hard when so many have been blinded and now realize what is wrong.

Then the next mechanism comes into play—forgive and forget. Not the way to go because you have not solved the problem. You have only sugar coated it and created some smoke and mirrors to reflect away what is truly there. A fight will constantly ensue because the grip of want, greed, materialistic desires and emotional crippling will continue to pervade this land.

We as a People have been fed many lies and now want to change all of it. The society of today thinks nothing of walking all over people with little thought in mind. What do you do when someone uncovers something that was said to be "truth?"

This is a very hard choice for someone to give up only to receive in the end. Think about it…can you give up all that you have to someone else and not feel anger. Anger not at the other but at those that created this illusion you now live. Living a lie is hard to give up…. it is hard to walk ones talk.

Many speak their words and never follow them. Most political leaders do this. They promise you the world and deliver you an empty plate. When you speak follow those words where they go. See if you really can take responsibility for those words. If you cannot then do not speak for you are tied to those words for many seasons to come.

Many do not feel they are living a lie. Many feel they are doing what they want to do and never really give it much thought. They go around living their lives as if nothing has happened and they are free of any responsibility from the past. They are not responsible for actions of the government and blame those around them, the people of the past and the politicians that serve them.

You cannot continue on the same path for long for eventually you see what is going on. You must rectify what you have supposedly done so blindly. The path you lead will depend on what you see and don't see. Living a lie should not be one of them.

Freedom

◆

Freedom…an illusion that is portrayed as something we have. The last "true" freedom that there was when our People lived upon the Plains. There wasn't anyone to tell you where to go. What to do. No fences to keep you out of Land that the Great Spirit owns. To watch all these people walking around thinking "man I've got a job, a brand new car, a nice place in the suburbs. I've got the life."

In my opinion you've been brainwashed. Do you think holding down a job that you go to day after day and do what the company wants you to do is freedom or even "financial" freedom? This is not freedom as freedom actually is. You can't move as quickly as would like because the company is paying your wage. Which, if you haven't forgotten, is paying for that new car, house and whatever else you've suckered yourself into buying. You are under the illusion you have freedom. And a true illusion it is.

Our People knew freedom like freedom was meant to be. You were free to roam as you pleased. You went anywhere without a lot of worries. You now have someone taxing you. There is always the possibility of your car not working or running out of gas. You never know whether or not you will survive an auto accident if you crash in one of these techno marvels. You need a job to maintain all of this and to get around. It's needed to keep your phone on, food on the table, heat in your home so you're not cold in the winter or on those chilly cool nights. We sure don't want your spa or Jacuzzi water getting cold now would we.

There is no such thing as freedom anymore. People are tied to something that holds them down. We cannot walk as we please anymore, anywhere we want or you will hear something to the effect of "get off my @%#*! land you moron" or "this is private property. Can't you read the signs or are you blind?" You walk on land "owned" by the park service or any other branch and your stuck with what rules they have in place. Only free to walk within the rules they have.

We as a People today do not know "true" freedom. Free from all this crap that is around us. The animals are no longer free. Only as free as their territory is or the person on that land allows. If someone will grant them the land to live on.

I am again reminded of this "illusion of freedom." The reality of lost freedoms and the illusion of what we think freedom is is what is present in this day and age. We all think we have freedom. We really don't. All smoke and mirrors within this society…all an illusion.

Enrollment

◆

I have seen long time good close friends destroyed because of this. Grandfather always said that he and grandmother refused to be included on this "enrollment list." They felt they knew who they were. They didn't need anyone telling them who they are. Especially the government. "When you look into the heart of a man or woman you will know who they are by their words and deeds…nothing else." These words still hold true today.

I had an Old One speak those same words and she was deeply saddened by this. I see the fun people poke at this issue. Some of it is well deserved by their actions. I have ties to people who have been destroyed by this issue as well as their families. I think we better look to maintaining our family and friendship ties rather than checking to see if facial features, skin color, number of blood cells in one's body, and all the other crap this issue brings forward, that the anthro's had to justify as to "what is an Indian."

The government is always trying to categorize things so it has better control of all the issues that we face. They see it as a way to control all that lives within its borders. When you try to do this you demean the whole process. I believe this is the whole intention. They are trying to define what an "Indian" is. There was never any definition until the Europeans set foot on this Land and tried to understand something that they had no idea of. They ran around amazed at all the "creatures" of the Land.

When they first came in contact with our People they had the gall to say they saw "savages" or "some kind of people, we're not sure what yet." I still laugh when the anthropologists talk about where the origin of the "first" People came from. This is a constant waste of precious resources for the sake of satisfying the whims of a few.

To try and think about the beginnings of time is like trying to think about what things will be like 2 billion years from now. You can predict forward and in the past but not when all the evidence is there. How can you even start to speculate when you really don't have a clue what happened back then? I know they have "education" but education also produces "educated idiots" instead of common sense. When you open yourself to the timeline of life you cannot just say, "ok, this is what is true and this is what is false." How can you possible think or believe that you know something or anything about anything. You don't. Our knowledge of what has been or what will be is like a half of a letter in an encyclopedia of about 300 volumes.

We have a lot of "know it alls" but very few who know what is really going on in this world. Enrollment is like belonging in a club. Is this what we are…a club? I think there is a definite loss of direction among our People. The government has tried to limit what is truly that of the People so that it will not have to pay out what is truly owed.

Enrollment is a smoke screen of the worst kind. Nowhere on this planet is there such a thing that exists among any other people. Those that want to limit who they think should belong to a Tribe or Nation are carrying it on. There is a constant attack on the integrity of a person. Who really cares if you are a half blood, a full blood or any blood in between. This belongs in the realm of the ego and should not even be among our People. It is constantly being fed to us by the agencies that want to limit and classify who we are as a people.

Musical Response

◆

You should sit and listen to the music of a quiet nature but Native none the less. Watch the backdrop of Nature doing its own thing at whatever movements it needs to afford survival for itself.

The clouds just flow to their own beat and with the Wind's direction and orchestration. Sometimes good, sometimes bad. The Winter's different shades of greens and browns soon to flip into the Spring Solstice. I sit here watching all this go on while others seem to walk and drive right by with little concept of what is going on around them. Or not even wanting to know.

I watch the animals and after a while they seem to start to move in orchestration to the music. Looking at this with rather odd thoughts of "what am I seeing". Am I listening to Nature's music with my own luck of the music playing or am I watching Nature responding to the music I am listening to? The birds flow through the breeze like a fish calmly moving through the stream with effortless movement. Giving in to its fluid movements. The deer were jumping over things as if never wondering what it is but just moving, as it should to get around obstacles. Young deer moving ever so limber. The blessing of youth.

Everything seems to move in orchestration to the music. But yet through all this I see that nature is always instilling its wisdom in whatever form we want to recognize. Everything in society is moving at a rat race pace. Never seems to slow down. Moving to the beat of nothing.

Nature trying to say, "Slow down." Allow the river life to flow through you. Sustain you on the surface. Never worrying about the undercurrent. Letting it just flow right past you.

Become graceful in your movements in life. Letting it flow by you like a fish within the stream. Not to worry about the obstacles. Just look at them and jump over them no matter how high they may be. All within the flow of the music. I sit here glad that nature is willing to listen to the music I play and allow me to flow within its wisdom and beauty. All in response to our own music but yet all within the same symphony.

The Tiniest of Them All

◆

I wonder at times why people sit around and talk, work, play or whatever else they are doing and completely ignore the world around them. I sit here looking at a group of ants and wonder why such a creature so small would be here. A creature so many people try to kill to get it out of their house or off "their" property. These thoughts of mine always seemed rather stupid around a lot of people I know. They think of me as some kind of lost minded lunatic that needs a mental hospital to reside in.

Why? I am not crazy for wondering about a creature so small that I feel a need to know why he came to be. The ant is a creature to be respected for all he does for our People, the other creatures on Mother Earth. Their interdependent skills allow for the disintegration of pieces of whatever is lying around for food for them so that nothing at all is ever wasted. Much like termites chew at the wood in the forest so that the nutrients from it will nourish our brothers and sisters in the Plant World.

Without these kinds of creatures to clean up after us, and chew it into nothing, we would have quite a mess on our hands. Their ways help other things to get nourishment. It is still yet another wonder of the integration of all living things together…including us. Why do people seem to feel that these creatures are so offensive and vial that they would kill them at any given moment? The age of trying to live a sterilized life is something of a wonder to me.

A doctor would perform surgery on the grass if need be for this is a very "clean" area to do so if he had to. Why? Some study proved this if it had to be then doing it there if there was no choice. Again.... why? With all the creatures living in that grass, on and under the grass why would they decide to do something such as this? Some say the Sun sterilizes the grass so that it becomes a "clean" surface.

Mother Earth is clean if left alone to its own ways. It cleans up after itself when it makes a mess. There are all kinds of creatures in this small world that have a job to do and a purpose to fulfill like the rest of us. We seem to be so ego driven, to a point of being suicidal, that we don't "see" the world around us. We "believe" we see but we really don't. We are "looking," not seeing. Do people worry when they lie down on the grass? Of course! They have visions of ants or bugs of some kind crawling in their expensive hairstyles and them screaming and running around like their back end was on fire.

If people "learn" to talk to these creatures there is no need for all these pesticides that chemical companies are making billions on. Chemical pollution is destroying everything in its wake. Scaring you into submission with their war of words against these so called "lowly" creatures. We also brag so much on how strong we are. These tiny creatures carry many times their weight. And do it quite well from my experiences so far with them. They have cleaned up many a mess without leaving a trace. Hmmm.... such lowly creatures? Not hardly. All of the Great Spirit's creatures have their place.

The Puddle and The Lake

◆

Does anyone ever think about the difference between a puddle and a lake? A puddle is something that in time disintegrates and is no longer there. While the lake continues to flow and do what it was taught to do. A puddle in time could become a lake with the right conditions, nourishment, and the right direction. Many lakes were puddles at one time and where able to grow to be what they are now. Our People relied on these lakes for the necessities of life. Its clean fresh water for drinking, bathing, cooking or just plain enjoyment of it.

We learned that lakes endure for a long time, were calm and yet ever flowing. They are ever changing. Even the subtleties were noticeable if you looked close enough. Many creatures relied on these lakes for their daily living. Many relied on it for many things.

The lake remained ever changing and yet stills itself. Knowing that many things relied on it for their survival it did all it can to hold and keep the balance as it could. The lake reflects the environment around it. It is still an integral part of everything around it. Maintaining the balance with all that is around. It enjoys being itself, going with the flow, shining at its best. Allowing input and giving output. Growing in the process. Both flowing in and out for the benefit of all. Animals of all kinds coming to drink from it shores.

Elk, deer, rabbits, foxes, bears and many others find its waters comforting. To swim within its fluid nature and never worrying about if its creatures are going to take advantage of it and pollute its life sustaining qualities.

When you stay like a puddle you will wither away and become nothing. Ever dependent on the things around you, down to the smallest thing. Even though it has expressed all it's energy to shine for one moment it is now no longer anything. It withers away in the sun and is gone. The puddle has all the ability to grow into a lake but its own flaws and shortcomings can make it no longer be if it doesn't grow and maintain a balance.

Now, some will think, but what if there is no more water to keep the balance and sustain itself. The Great Spirit knows what we "need" to keep ourselves in balance. We will be shown things that will "keep" the balance for us. Some are good and some not so good. If our arrogance gets in the way then bad things will happen to knock us down to size. That is why a balance must be maintained so that bad things will not happen except that which Mother Earth seems fit to occur within its own balancing.

Like the puddle there would no longer be anything here. Something that was but is no more.

Balance

———————— ◆ ————————

Balance is something that is on everyone's mind. It seems that some try to conquer it but never really succeed. They think they do but they are only kidding themselves. There are others that just look to see if there is a balance. If not, so what, nothing I can do. Then there are the others that try and work at trying to understand. They try to be a part of it but intellectualize too much and eventually lose it.

Finally there are those that just allow things to be as things are and let it work itself out. They learn from the animals and all around themselves. These are my People, Native Peoples. We always try to learn a balance in all things that are, both within and without our lives. We do not try to overcome it by conquering it. We sit there and try to understand what it is, it is trying to tell us. We also learn by mistakes like all living things on Mother Earth.

Trial and error is a learning tool everyone learns by no matter who or what we are or where we are sitting at the moment. Nature can take care of itself rather nicely without anyone's intervention. You cannot go around and say, "I'm going to do what is best for Mother Earth and help all I can." This is a poor way of looking at it. Mother Earth already knows what to do. It doesn't need our intervention unless we have caused damage to the point of no return. If this happens you better work like hell because your about to die right along with all other living creatures that eat, live and breathe on this planet.

Balance is known by but a very few people. Educated people seem to think they know where this "balance" is. They take all their knowledge and try to rationalize what this "balance" is. How do you know what balance is if you have never seen it work?

The only thing we see when balance is there is the effect of getting out of balance. So then, how can you tell then if you are "out of balance?"

Within our Lands there are many interactions that occur. So many in fact that we are amazed by the vastness of them. There is an easier way but it can only be learned by someone knowledgeable in this and knows where that balance lies.

Balance is just the ability to look at the circle and see what needs to be fixed. Without this sight balance is very hard to maintain. It is like trying to see through the darkness with sunglasses on.

Old Ways of the Ancestors

$\blacklozenge$

In life there is a lot that goes on that is a result of ones actions of the Past. That result may not be what we like to see.

As I walk this path I see most who don't have the time to follow what should still be done as was done by our Ancestors. This will not work in this day and age. It was different back then. We're more modern now…so they say. A lot of superstitions and myths…so they say again.

The Ancestors lived a freedom that none of us may ever know or feel. This was destroyed by invasions of people who thought they were doing what was right for our people. And still try to to this day.

Do we "really know" what is going on around us? I believe most do not. They think they do but this is a false sense of knowing. This is the sad part. We rely on these wonderful machines to tell us what the Ancestors taught as oral tradition. The ability to "see" is being lost so fast that it will die a quick death.

The Ancestors are restless to a point that they speak daily. But very few are "truly" listening. They think it is a figment of his/her imagination but it is not. We all sit around looking for things to make us who and what we are…. why? What is all the waiting about? How can you wait for a train that is long gone with no arrival time even in sight?

Arguments are for the foolish. We lose our way daily because we fall into this trap. It is continual for some reason. Is learning beyond the capacity of many in this world or have we become reactionaries with no time to "actually" think?

The wonders of listening to the old ones and their stories are a daily trip down the road of history. So why ignore it? Why put energy into something that will only drain you? The future is based on today's path. The act of listening is a lost art. To listen to the story and allow it to work its way through you for clarification into "your" life is no longer there.

Why are we so bent on finding something to secure ourselves to? Are we that insecure as a People to allow this to continue on? ii am amazed at all the people who say they are this or that when they really have no idea who they are as an Native. What ever happened to the depth that we were at one time?

Like the old saying always driven into me…"still waters run deep but never stagnant."

I sat here the other night to the early hours of the morning watching a 10 point buck and his family and a family of skunks with a couple of raccoons sitting in this yard eating to their hearts content. Even though the raccoons were tearing the garbage to bits. I was watching this circle of life before me. Such a good thing to watch. The wonders of all life.

What is "really" important in this life to each person is different. To me, the Circle and all its stories, traditions, and respect for all life is what is important to me. T he Old Ways of the Ancestors.

The Wind and the Cetan (Hawk)

◆

Many days ago I sat here finally outside in the sun when it is not so cold. I started to feel one with the Winged Ones, Four-Leggeds and Mother Earth. I sat gliding with the two hawks that showed up today after a bit of an absence. Gliding with them on the wind and feeling the gentle breeze beneath the wings. Feeling better from the weight of many issues going on. Feeling their power and gentleness and the feelings they were feeling. One of being close to the Great Spirit, the Wind and Mother Earth. All in unity together. The Cetan has watched over many trips I have traveled across these lands. Flying close by or sitting there watching as I go by.

Today was different though because I got a closer glimpse of their wisdom and power. Feeling of being so close to the Wind as it flows through these feathers. A stronger bond of respect I have gained from it. A feeling that I am never alone within the Great Spirit's world. The Four-Leggeds in their wisdom and power teach us many things. They will always guide and take care of needs that have to be met. The pair of them, the hawks flowing so free without the worries we have. Sometimes there are senseless worries. The feeling of gentleness the wind brings when flowing through. The whisper of its voice. The Wind and the Cetan together. Both are very powerful but are ever so gentle. Ever watching and flowing as carefree as can be. The ancestors and the Creator watch through their eyes. Ever watching our moves and guiding those that are willing to watch and listen to their teachings.

Today I sit here watching a Cetan solitary float on the Wind with the snow traveling by its wings. It was a gentle breeze. Not like days that have past where the wind has flowed much harder due to weather changes occurring. He flowed ever so freely on the Wind, seemingly suspended there without anything holding him place. His head moved slowly side to side looking for what he could find to find himself and his family.

The hawk…he stands for swiftness and endurance. He is able to fly over large areas of the land in search for things to eat or build a nest. He moves in a quick and silent manner so that no one knows he is coming. His spirit is strong. He teaches many things to us if we listen close enough to allow those things to sink in. His spirit is mysterious but known to those that listen and hear his words of wisdom.

As with all things in nature and on mother earth the feelings I felt with them is something I don't think I could ever put to words but that feeling is welcomed anytime with my brother the hawk. The respect that is due to them and the wisdom they impart is something that must be felt and experienced.

The Deer and
the Gifts They Leave

◆

The deer is A Four-Legged that is a wonder to watch and see within its own environment. I walked one day not long ago, the normal route I walk to get the mail. The mailbox being a quarter mile away from the house I would walk back and stubble across something that was not there the countless many times I have walked this path down the hill.

The kids walked with me many times enjoying the sunshine and playing along the way. On our half mile round trip to the mailbox sometimes for nothing more than the usual junk mail that seems to permeate this small home. The day seemed no more out of the ordinary than any other. Four-Leggeds doing their normal thing as they usually do. We stopped to pet the horses after the youngest calls to them and they come running to greet us. On the way back up the hill that seems at times to be one of the most tiring to climb, we walk our route up to the house with our usual stampede of footsteps that the young ones create during their endless stream of energy.

In the time even before this the deer came around with great frequency to this small place in the mountains. They ate here and slept here. The males would do their ritualistic maneuvers around mating season. The old ones, the parents, the teenagers and young ones are all together within their own clan. All of them enjoyable to watch as they move around the forest and prairie. I watched with an interest that grew and has grown ever so closely as time has passed.

My appearance to them after a while seemed less of a threat and seemed not to bother them anymore. There was a bonding I could feel but not explain nor verbalize. As I walked up the path back to the house I came across something I had not expected to see. I looked at it and wondered where it came from. It was not there a short time ago when we walked down this path.

Why is it here now? I picked it up and brought it home. When I picked it up there was something that was quite different. It made my hands tingle like they haven't before. I knew about this but wondered why now. Grandfather had told me things like this would occur and that it meant the object is sacred and would help create a connection to those that left it. Since that day my life has changed in a way I never thought would occur in my lifetime.

A connection I still do not understand but respect highly and am learning daily about. A gift I could never repay to them. A gift that allows me to see into their world and experience it first hand as one of them and not as a spectator. A world unlike our own but very similar. A gift I also thank the Creator for. A world that is transforming me more than I would ever have thought of. The gift of the deer.

The River

———————— ◆ ————————

The river is a living being the flows ever so gently to a destination at the end of its journey. It flows so freely and carelessly through the land. You walk in it and feel it's power and gentleness. The river has a soothing ability to flow away the problems in this everyday rat race of ours. It flows without pretense. It opens itself to all that need it for survival. Its life giving energy found within its boundaries is enormous. It helps all to survive around it.

The trees near the banks, the fish, the Four-Leggeds, everything needs its nourishment in all forms. As it flows by you, you gain a sense of oneness with it. Whether you're swimming in it, floating in it or just sitting on its banks, you watch the river flow by with a gentleness that enters your spirit. The hawks swoop down to catch fish for its young that will one day flow above its water on the wind…another river of a different kind. The river is an abundance of life for all to see if you look closely enough at it. Its life is every flowing outward from its center.

Each river, stream, lake puddle, ocean, whatever, has its character and life that it sends to all creatures. As you sit on the bank watching it, feeling it, listening to its ever-flowing nature your presence becomes ever embraced by its life. A life that never ends and keeps going without end. We must be on constant guard of the water that surrounds us for it is what keeps us alive. It keeps us alive not only in body but in our mental, emotional and spiritual lives. It flows through every part of out being to fulfill the needs of each.

The animals need its gifts. The plants, the fish, all creatures need it. So tell me why people pollute these rivers, streams, oceans, lakes, any body of water. It all comes around to us. The Circle always completes its task. It always comes back to the beginning. Haunted we will be by the continual flow of chemicals that pollute these waters and suck the life from it. It is a living being. It is just as important as than you or me. What do have to gain by having a green lawn without weeds? I use this term loosely because there is no such thing as weeds.

Many botanists will tell you differently that there is no such thing. This perception is one of bigotry towards nature. To keep one and get rid of the other just because we do not like it and do not want it around makes no sense at all. Many think this is a trivial point. Think of it this way. What if you, your child or anyone for that matter goes to work, school or has just been born. You sit there and say, "Oh you are such a good baby."

Now, what if someone else does not like it and decides "This baby will not grow up to be useful so lets get rid of it." Does that sound trivial now? You would probably sit there and say, "This guy is nuts, where does he get off deciding this?" "Where does he get off relating a plant, animal or any creature to a baby?" I am sure there is any number of thoughts occurring right now. Well you know, that is how I see it. Nothing is any better or any worse than anything else. Human, plant, animal, it, thing, whatever, it doesn't matter. It makes no difference. Life is life, no matter what it is.

Everything alive has a purpose…everything. Many will not see it this way because their life's experiences tell them differently. Your senses, mind, emotions, thoughts, everything tells you differently. They are like the river. They flow constantly through you without an end. The river is ever flowing towards another destination. You see things that you think are there but your senses have fooled you into thinking this is what is true and what is right. The river is a gift for us, to mull around. It allows us think about things that we need to see clearly.

It allows us to move our river so it does not become stagnant. The physical river is tied to the river within us. They both flow towards a common goal and meet eventually at the end, wherever that end may be. It is important for us to preserve our water in whatever form it flows in. If it should die then so shall we. We are tied to it no matter what. Its life is our life and our life is its life.

When a deer drinks from the stream it drinks from its life source as well as from others. It plays in the stream much like we do. It is a wonder to watch the young ones jump around like toys with spring legs. Frolicking about with seemingly endless amount of energy.

Their young minds exploring the river and all that live there. Watching fish go by and wonder "what's that thing?". Standing there also looking at its reflection and asking themselves who that is…"ah someone to play with." The river is an endless source of amusement, energy, life and interactions. It would be a shame to lose that, which gives us so much life as well as many others. It is a constant source of life-giving properties. A part of the same river we all belong to. The river of life. Think about it.

Mother Earth

◆

When people think they are a part of Mother Earth do they really think that they are? Or is this a cloud that sits in their mind? I have seen many people run around proclaiming they are this and that they are that in/with nature. Hmmm. I never know what to think about these people.

Mother Earth is a large entity with many parts. To become a part of something you already are is something of a sideshow for me. People run around saying, "I am a part of Mother Earth and I feel good about it" or "I love being a part of nature for it is so wonderful." We as a People know we are already a part of it. We are all of it and it is all of us. We are it and it is we. How ever you want to say it. You can never be apart from it or get away from it. It is like being an air molecule and trying to get away from the air. It is rather ludicrous don't you think?

Mother Earth is a living breathing spirit that encompasses all that live within it. When you pollute it you are polluting your bloodstream, your lungs, your body. So I have yet to understand why people continue to do this. Mother Earth is not an endless circle of pollution sucking machine. It WILL breakdown and then we will see things that no person has seen in the history of this planet.

Mother Earth is a living being. It is not something that is abused at a whim and thrown out when ever we feel like it. This is where we live and where all our children for many generations to come will be living and raising their children.

Mother Earth is a self-contained ecosystem that has a balance within the spirit it possesses. The land is an interaction that moves in a world of constant change. Everything is in a constant balance all over her. As she gives birth she takes away life. Today there is an out of balance within her. As the world grows so do the problems she exhibits. Those problems are getting bigger each day.

People are creating more problems then they are solving. There is an imbalance that will come that will be like no other imbalance before us. The spirit of the land has to balance or trouble ensues. Sometimes the balance we think should be is not what Mother Earth has in mind. We need to aggressively stop all this and reverse our position before we have reached the point of no return. Time is running out.

In That Moment

◆

Tonight I sit here reliving a situation I was in such a short time ago that it still lives like this moment as I speak. We all tend to argue at a moment's notice but it makes little sense to do so. I had the privilege of knowing a couple of long ages. Eighty's or ninety's…I cannot remember. In the situation I am about to spoke of age meant very little to anyone.

I was trying to heal an individual with multiple problems going on the same time. She was small with only a small amount of muscle left on her weary and aged bones. The spouse sat quietly at her side with a calmness I have not felt for over 30 years. The calmness was like a dream of lying by the lake on a sunny day. You have no cares what so ever. The clouds are floating by with no more direction than a gentle breeze moving about the trees changing directions at a whim.

He sat there with little more than a smile on occasion. As time moved on she had an unfortunate turn that sent her onto live support. He watched with a tireless smile I have never seen before. I started to become intrigued with this couple and how each other before this supported each with a caring attitude not ever seen before by me. The gentleness of their nature was something I felt all the way through to my spirit and deeper. It started to encompass me like a robe but not heavy. It resembled a mist in the spring that hangs low along the prairie before being burned off by the morning sun. As I tried with all the power given to me to save her from the grips of death, I saw a lot more in that moment than in any year in my life. Before this I had the opportunity to sit down and talk with him.

His voice was as gentle as newborn baby's skin, as gentle as the hair on a newborn animal. So gentle it permeated all aspects of my mind...like a sharp knife cutting away anything in its path. He spoke of all the things that happened in their lives...both good and bad. He spoke of their meeting and how they became part of each other. He spoke of the many arguments they had and many of the finer moments of their life. He spoke with gentleness that at times seemed to unnerve me. I wondered how a couple could go their so much pain, suffering, losses of all kinds and still maintain gentleness like this.

Grandfather and grandmother both spoke of this and had this gentleness through their many talks. Despite my constant energies to hold onto her life and keep her above water she started down the road where others were waiting for her to go to the ancestral ground. Slowly she slipped away. She started walking the last path to those friends and family and where she will meet her spouse when he passes into the ancestral world. He watched with a smile and gentleness unknown. He watched her breath slowly slip away. He watched in a way that I knew he was well aware of. I also stood there with him on that path but I had uneasiness.

With all the death I have seen this was a totally different set of emotions. The gentleness permeated the room as her life slipped completely away from this life. His gentleness seemed then a very welcomed relief. Every day I struggle with life and death situations. His gentleness was nothing I had ever felt before since my early years. He was smiling with a gentle smile of knowing that one day soon he would see her again and be with her for a very long time after that. I stood there with a grief and tears inside I could not bear at times. His gentleness seemed to help hold me back from expressing what I truly felt about this seemingly unknown couple to me before this.

In that moment the gift of the deer sank into my mind and into my spirit. It sank in with a gentleness I have always wanted to feel but because of all the things that permeated my life I was unable to stay within that gentleness and hold it. In that moment he looked up from her and smiled at me and said, "Son, we have lived a life that we both enjoyed no matter what happened. Sometime soon I will join her and we will both be able to walk the green grass of the meadows together.

We will climb the mountains and sit there watching the views of all around us. To be angry about anything is foolish. If you go to bed angry what then? If you pass in the night with that will you be able to live with yourself? Will you be able to meet your friends and family with a clearness of heart? It is not worth wasting your time on such wasteful thoughts. Live so that you will walk the road of gentleness and your days will never be cloudy. The sun will always shine." In that moment I was totally speechless. I looked at him with no thoughts in my mind at all. I stood there within his gentleness of heart and spirit. In that moment I learned what these deer around me have been trying to speak for some time now. Standing there within their quiet nature, their gentle heart. In that moment I learned that harsh emotions bring pain and suffering. Only gentleness of the heart will get you through anything.

If there is nothing pushing on the door the wrong way then the door is easier to open. I prayed to the Creator that day for this man to cross over with little pain and the welcoming of friends and family to greet him. To this day I have not heard from him but still think of those words and how all things finally tied together. In this moment I still remember his gentleness of the heart.

Walking the Red Road

◆

When we walk a path we walk from point to point. Whether it is red, white, black or whatever. Solving problems as we go. Each path follows like all things in life a pattern due to our events of the past. Some of those events are good and fulfilling others are bad and we would rather forget we even had them. The Canku Luta (red path) is appealing to many due to its simplicity and closeness to the Creator when we follow our true path and not one of money, greed, vanity and many others here I would rather not mention.

If one comes to a path that is not of their color should that person be told to go back to their original path and see if it is right and then come back? They would not be here if that path was correct for them. Hmmm. This is a hard question to answer especially when we have not seen the path that they left or what guided them to this point in time and to this path. Many have walked this white road and are vary dissatisfied with this way.

Do we have the total right to say, "This is our path? You have no rights here so go back to your own path and find wisdom there first before you come to ours". I believe we do not have the "exclusive right" to tell someone this. The Creator is one to all no matter of color, ways, and background, ect. What I have found is that we as a People are becoming as prejudice against others as we are against our own brothers and sisters. Why?

The more one fights a wall the more it does not move. It becomes harder out of defiance. Wisdom and education is what is needed. People are here for a reason. They have come here to learn why we are how we are and try and make their own lives more simple and honorable. As we go down our path as a people we are losing our own sights because of all the side tracking. I maintain my way no matter what society says. No matter who or what may cross my path. No two paths can ever be mixed. Ever. Causes great confusion within our lives.

All paths cross at some point for it is inevitable. When we speak of asking someone to follow his or her own path what decision are we making? Are we not practicing a small part of bigotry? You stay over there and I will stay over here? We are not right for you or you for us. No one can make this decision for some one else. It seems I learned somewhere that we cannot tell another how or what to do with their life. Has this been forgotten? It seems it has been.

Journey on the Edge of a Storm

◆

A few days ago I decided, after a very strong push to do so, to take a trip to the high desert and get reoriented back to mother earth. I left this illogical world behind along with the entire electronic hubbub as well.

I started on a 1500-mile trek that would take me into another area of the land I have not been in before. The weather here was as gorgeous as ever and I left as soon as I could. Once about half way through the drive I started to hit the passes in order to get to the high desert. These same passes I would have to travel on my way back.

On arrival to the high desert the temperature though increased to 95 degrees in the morning, a temperature in the high country equal to the low hundreds at sea level. The sun was intense like no other day I have experienced to this day. It reminded me of walking on the sand dunes at mid-day, very hot and dry. But I continued on my drive down into the canyons some 13 miles below.

The road was very dry and dusty. Rocks strewn all over and this car were not made for such travels into the deep recesses of mother earth. Continual maneuvering was constantly needed to get around all the rocks. The road twisted like a snake through the canyons while the canyon walls started their climb straight up towards the deep blue sky…up towards the Creator. In this area the ancestors carved their writings on the walls to leave a road map of what they saw and experienced in their days many centuries ago...a good reminder of the old ways and their hidden messages present there.

I stopped for a short time to feel the words under my hands and feel their life spring forward through these writings. Their writings, which many see as rather "primitive", but were rather advanced because they have endured centuries and are still around to speak their words and message even today. The message streams forward even though many see them as something mysterious and foreboding.

I move on after my visit with the Ancestors and reliving some of their messages. I traveled further down the canyons watching the road disappear behind me in a cloud of dust and sand. As I get closer to the bottom the area starts to become greener. The streams present at the bottom of this high desert weave their cool waters around these canyons...a feast for any weary traveler crossing it path.

At the same time I began to wonder what the trip would be like back up these canyons in the bright sun of the day. Would the car overheat in this sun leaving all stranded in the hot sun? Hmmm. I thought. Not something I really would like to happen at this point or really any point in time of my life.

It continued on despite these thoughts of uncertainty. Something was pulling me down to the bottom of these canyons despite the precarious nature of the trip down. As arrival at the bottom was not far away I saw old hogans or some type of clay-covered structure sitting by itself but yet a very integral part of this land. Sitting very quietly upon the land but not an intrusion like so many things that I see. A very quiet member of this place.

At the bottom finally I got out to look around and the canyon walls flew their slick walls towards the Creator and their colors showed brightly in the mid-day sun. The trees, grass and all other members of the plant families rustled gently in the gentle breeze. The stream weaved it way down through these canyon walls. I saw a rather odd site here as well. A flock of Canadian geese were following these waters somewhere but I didn't have a clue. It is very unusual to see Canadian geese on the high desert. This area is very dry and hot with little food present for many, many miles in all directions. I wondered at this site and wondered if I was not in the same boat as my winged friends. Following a feeling from what I know but not knowing where that path will lead…feeling misplaced so to speak. A rather interesting correlation I thought…. what else is the Creator going to tell me on this trip.

I sat there for some time listening to the water flow on its way to some unknown destination and feeling its flow as a part of this canyon despite the dryness and heat present all around. Everything is an integral part of each other and each reliant on the other for support and life itself. All this reminding me of how much people of all races are destroying the land as fast as they can without any insight to seeing how when you destroy one aspect or throw it out of balance you disrupt the whole and things start happening.

I sat there wondering why people just don't wake up. Why are they so blinded by greed, dishonesty, ego, arrogance and anything else you could imagine? There is no smoke and mirrors here…only life. Life as it truly is. Me being me. The plants being who they are. The water being who it is. Everything being itself. No pretensions, no nothing. A rather simple way I thought of living life. So what is the problem with people then?

So much confusion I think through out our daily lives. The constant barrage of electronic bull all around us. The constant barrage of having to strive for something when in fact you strive for nothing…nothing of any value anyway.

I stayed for a while and enjoyed the soothing world here of mother earth. I started back up the hill out of this oasis of life towards the high desert again. The sun at its peak and the heat stifling to say anything at all. I stuck with the ol' ijun air-conditioning…. open windows. The dryness was enough to choke any raindrop of its life. The dryness so dry that the carcass of a pronghorn was raised partly off the ground at each end…a rather gristly site. A reminder of what happens when you are weak and can't make it to water.

It also reminded me of what happens when we cut ourselves as a people off from the Creator.

Moving back up the canyons through these snake-like turns becomes at times precarious for this car. It's inability to clear enough a lot of the sand and gravel on this road. This same road that if it rains even a small amount becomes impassable. Another thought rang through my mind at this point. What if by reputation a rainstorm came suddenly over these canyon walls from any direction? Instant stranded I said. It reminded me of the suddenness things can happen here within the vast mountains and canyons. The unpredictability that happens and catches so many people within these mountains…. many to their deaths due to lack of knowledge of these majestic peaks, canyons and valleys and lack of being prepared properly for sudden changes.

Out of these canyons I drove with a bit of prayer on my breath. Wanting the car to make it through the heat and sun and up from the womb of mother earth. The dust and sand coating the car like paint. The temperature of the car rising higher as the car rose higher up the canyon. Thoughts of being stranded in the desert rang through but then I thought would this really happen…why? I believe it was the Creator who brought me to this place and he would not allow me to get stranded here. I was asked to come here. I was a little more confident but kept my sacred pouch close to me anyway just in case I was wrong.

After much chugging and snaking through these canyons I made it up to the top of these majestic peaks. I looked back at the road taken and said one day I will return to enjoy more of your beauty. Back to the civilized road now I drove back. Back from a two-day stay among these friends of mine. As I drove down the road clouds started to come together in their usual fashion of an impending storm. Lucky I thought to be out of the canyon. Hmmm….not such a good thought after all. I would end up riding the edge of a storm all the way home.

The storm continued to brew and gather strength before my eyes. The site was something to see but I was nervous at its presence. Such dark clouds gathering in front of me. I continued on for these mountains and passes are unpredictable and maybe it will shift direction to another path. Ha…not likely. The storm started shooting lightning in all directions. Hell I thought…now what.

The lightning blasted burn spots all over. I stopped at some to make sure they weren't going to become major fires in the making. Some spots where lightning hit had spots 30 x 60 feet burned. Yikes! My eyes grew. I have never seen lightning strikes so large. I was not liking what I was seeing nor getting into. The storm gathered all around. The rain was scattered almost as much as the lightning was. The bolts battered the ground with such brute force it even bothered me.

Back into the car I got and down the road I flew in hopes of getting around this storm that was making me a bit nervous. I was already into the passes and had to keep going for civilization was few and far between. The dark clouds and lightning were definitely not a good sign…. especially in a very dry area where forest fires can start quickly and catch you off guard.

As I was going through an 11,000-foot pass and starting down the other side when a split occurred in the clouds. I have seen clouds move from one direction to another due to the mountain peaks and changes in wind direction but this was a little different. I was still on the edge of the storm. Seeing and feeling its effects but not within it…no longer in it. I continued driving down the mountain watching the storm horseshoe around me. I have seen a lot of different things but this most definitely rates near the top.

Throughout the rest of the trip the storm stayed in this pattern…no matter what direction we took or way the passes turned. I have seen weather changes but this is something else. I kept driving regardless of this sight. As I drove the clouds threw their lightning in all directions lighting up the sky. Darkness started to fall and the travel continued on it's wet way but this car saw no rain on its windshield. As I got closer to civilization the storm slowly dissipated and disappeared after going through the last pass.

Finally arriving home I got out and looked at the night sky. It was clear and the stars shown ever so brightly…so many of them twinkling in the night sky. Just then I felt a touch on my left shoulder but no one was there. Just then I looked up at the night sky and saw shooting stars cross the night sky.

The only thing I could do at that point was smile. I thanked the Creator for such a learning experience and thanking him for showing me his wonders and being a part of them. Helping me to relax more despite the turmoil going on around me in this world. Really nothing compared to the wonders he can make…everything of ours seems so trivial.

I thanked him for this whole journey on the edge of a storm.

Journey Across the Divide

◆

The journey across the divide is not an easy one. When one walks the road to another place or person that person must know how to follow. Must know how to walk behind and beside it as you walk along. When you walk along the path…the path in between…it is a path not known to many. Not known to those that think they know what is going on. Some just call it some kind of mysticism but it is far from it. There are many who seem to think they know the way. These people only fall into the abyss. They fall where the clouds end and the sky begins. To see what is there is not possible with the human eyes or ears for nothing is seen nor heard.

Many things occur here but nothing in relation to what you see. There are many who are crossing this divide but they see nothing present there. No relationship between anything. They abuse all they can but know little of what they do. Blindness unto itself and to other things and people. We seem to think we know all that is needed to know and take all we can without regards to where the balance lies, where the middle ground of all things lie. As we cross our lives we cross many things that stop along our path. We view these things with contempt with little regard as to why they are there, as to their purpose on your path.

When you walk across this area where all things as well as nothing exists where are you thinking you are going. Mother Earth creates all creatures to live in balance so that no one thing ever gets in front of the other. They are all equal with no one ever getting ahead. The animals that live here are here for their purpose as well as ours but not for the food chain alone. We as a human race seem to think we are superior to all things when in fact we know little to nothing about anything. We cross other's paths with little to no knowledge of anything of what they are or do and pass judgment like we are the Creator.

The divide shows little mercy to anyone and takes any that care to surrender to its vast breadth. It is so wide but yet so thin. It takes little to cross if the knowledge is there to traverse its great size. Like traversing a great ocean or sifting through a fog that has occurred. When we fail we feel like we are nothing but yet we continue on.

The spirits that lie within this area are helpful in all ways possible but we must first gain their confidence and then they will move with us to solve our problems. Our arrogance is what causes our failures to occur. Not our lack of knowledge. Once we step outside our arrogance we will see more that we've ever wanted.

This divide is not some fairy tale that you are brainwashed into believing. It is the area where all things must cross. The area where confusion meets understanding. Where we all stand when watching our lives move forward on our path.

As we move closer our journey is made easier and acceptance is not far away.

Weather

◆

The weather is an ever-constant changing mass of molecules and energy that shift constantly and at times without notice. To change it is both simple and complex. To move air masses around the molecules must move precisely the path that will accomplish what is at the end of that path. Cloud formation and destruction are two forms that come from the same mix. Moving molecules and energy along a path too quickly can cause great harm and many uncertainties. The mix of hot or warm air with that of cold to make rain is known but the mechanisms for making it happen remain secret. Only to be used as needed and for dire necessity.

The Great Spirit helps by allowing their formation to take place. The Spirits of the Four Directions help by assisting. The collision of two paths cannot run too quickly for lightning, tornadoes and possibly hurricanes can form. Hurricanes need the oceans to form along with a regular supply of water and churning effect to continue their circular path. Very few have yet to understand the reason hurricanes maintain an eye. It is a rather simple idea but eludes many.

The movement of a storm or even a shower has a particular character due to the path it has to take to form. Some people say there is an imbalance that occurs in order for a storm to occur. This cannot be farther from the truth. As clouds float by, they move on a path much as we do. They are constantly changing to keep up with the times and change many ways before reaching their destination. That is why there are so many different kinds of clouds. Many say it is due to the chemical makeup and the surroundings that make these clouds. Each one has a character all it own and joins with others when the time is right.

There are many types and kinds of weather as there are levels. Each level has its own particular kind of weather or storms. Some are subtler than others. From the surface to the outer atmosphere there are many levels and many types of weather. The molecules move differently in each level. When too much movement occurs in one level it moves its way down to the lowest, ground level so to speak. Many are seeing the effects like depletion of the ozone level near the top of the earth.

There are many levels being affected in between. As a result of the changing character of these levels the air movement around the Mother Earth is changing and causing lower level air movement to occur. All the levels interact with each other. One level causes change in another. Subtle changes in all these levels are causing changes in the magnetic fields of Mother Earth.

Mother Earth is an electric field with constant changes occurring on all levels. These electric fields are much like our fields that are around us. Both are changing within and on the outside of our bodies. Both are ever changing for good or bad. Weather is the effect of the changing magnetic and electric fields changed by physical and other means.

The government is trying to make, or should I should say already has a device that causes earthquakes to occur. It changes the magnetic field thus causing shaking to occur. Weather movements are dynamic so if you think that controlling them is possible, think again. The different levels are in constant change and when changing one level you change others that will cause a boomerang effect. What goes out must come back. That is why we as natives have learned about the circle and how it works. All life and what we do returns to us at some point. You can never get away from it. Weather is the same way.

Alter it and the effects may not be what you planned. Our constant polluting of the air, water, ground and everything else we are causing dramatic and deadly changes not seen yet. There is only so much Mother Earth can do to counteract these pollutants but the pollution outweighs the mechanisms to change it or neutralize it. The changes will cause a drastic shift to the far end causing many changes to occur throughout all the ecosystems and levels of the atmospheres.

Think of a pond or lake. You are constantly dumping crap into it on a regular basis. It does not take a rocket scientist to know what will happen. Eventually it will kill all things in it and remain that way until changes occur to eliminate the toxins and support life again.

It will take quite a long time to change the damage being done right now. Each level from the ground up to the outer most atmosphere all move at different speeds and energy levels. Changes can occur in minutes to days of altering. Some slight changes can go too far and cause massive earth changes to occur. Mother Earth is in a constant state of balancing. What happens on one side must balance somewhere else. Top to bottom, right to left, left to right, bottom to top, doesn't matter. Both sides are reacting to maintain balance. Each of the Four Directions has a purpose and must do what they can to balance Mother Earth. Each direction causes changes. This I think we already know.

The Shifting of Mother Earth to keep the seasons in balance is a necessity that has to be maintained. Without the seasons great changes will occur in the microscopic world. There will an unbalancing of microbes around Mother Earth. The microbes would take advantage of this. Many diseases would run rampant that were curbed by the freeze-thaw effect. If this is not maintained then long term problems occur. Such diseases that were controlled by this and by barrier would then become loose and wreak havoc where they once were not. We may not like when diseases run rampant with no way of stopping them. The sneeze of someone could cause death to occur in others.

Without the balance of the weather our future remains gloomy at the least. Mother Earth can only shift for so long and balance things for so long until she tires and lets go. When she does we will know the effects rather well and will remember them for centuries to comes.

The Heart of the Land

◆

Many seem to think they know how to "manage" the land. There is no such thing. Your lack of knowledge regarding **all** segments of the land is what causes you and others harm. There are many spirits that help concerning managing the land. Each one has a job as we do in the physical. The Plant, Stone and Mineral Nations each with their own job to do. Each supports another and plays a part in it. The animals and insects all have their parts to play within an ecosystem. Some say that we can do it without this one or that but this is a falsehood.

The heart of the land is a separate part but still a part of the whole ecosystem. It plays a very big part in it. Much like the Creator is to us. Without him we would not be here or exist. The heart of the land is the soul of the land. Once you destroy it, it takes a long time to return to it normal state.

The constant destruction of the land is becoming a problem for the many creatures that inhabit the land. We dig the land for pools, houses, golf courses, commercial development and the like and destroy the very essence of the land as it once was.

I have found that within this heart most things survive great travesties. They recover without much difficulty if allowed to do so. There has been survival from great fires and earthquakes that have rocked turtle island. Young sprouts come to life and renew it. All creatures that live on the land contribute towards this heart of the land.

To feel this you must go out and become a part of it. You must become accepted onto and into the land. The heart will open slowly only when it knows it can trust you. Once trusted with this knowledge the wonders Mother Earth opens. The wisdom of the land comes forward. If you betray the trust of the land and the creatures that live upon it the trust will never be. It will take a very long time for you to become accepted again.

Once the heart of a land becomes destabilized and broken it will die. It will take a long time for that area to return to its normal ways.... if it ever does. The heart of the land, as I mentioned before, is something that is unseen but still very much alive and present. The feel of an old growth forest is different from a new one with very new trees in it. It is this feel that expands to all creatures on the land. Once the "experience" and "older life" becomes destroyed, the land is different from how it was before. It is like when a company would fire all it's older employees in favor of the young ones with no experience because they are cheaper to employ. These younger employees know little of the revelations and hard spots that occur and only can experience take you through these hard times. Nothing...I mean nothing replaces experience in anything we do.

The same occurs on Mother Earth. The experience of the land can never replace anything else. When you kill off all the older things then there is nothing there to teach the younger ones have to live and make them strong. The land remains intertwined together. To continue on the current path of destruction will only cause Mother Earth to fail and then the death of us all or a large portion of us. I do not think we really want to sit here and watch our lives slowly whither away when there is no food anywhere, no water to drink. All due to the cycle of water being interrupted or corrupted by other factors and leading to an acceleration of normal processes.

The land within it has a spirit that permeates all things and causes much interconnection to occur. Without this interconnection the living things within it will die.

The Bridge

◆

Tonight for the first time I realized where the bridge lies between here and the spirit world. It is difficult to explain how our ceremonies work and the connection they give between me and that of the Great Spirit. That connection is different than that of any other path or road taken and between each person. Unless you are truly native you may not understand this. Grandfather spoke of a connection that binds but yet is not visible. It is only visible when trust is formed between you and the spirit. Whether it is the land or anything else.

This has no connection whatsoever to the new age mumbo jumbo that has taken some of our people and blinded them to the spirituality of their ancestors. I sat and watched an elder sit by herself but was quite content within the world she was in.

She displayed the trust of that world and all the plants, animals, insects, ect. Around her. She had little to fear from anything around her and displayed this confidence in a quiet manner.

I thought I had seen the strong connection between our people and the spirit but I was wrong. Tonight I had the opportunity to step a little farther onto this bridge and see what he was speaking about.

Nothing can take place unless the heart is in the right place and the other accepts that trust is in turn. It is much like friendships and relationships. As growth occurs a bridge is built between you...one of trust and heart.

Without this nothing can take place and nothing can move forward the way you want. This plays a significant roll in the trust relationship we have with the land. We as a people are a bridge to that world so that Mother Earth can heal.

I sit and watch all these sites both native and non-native declare what they think they know about the connection of who and what we are as a people. They bring in all this new age stuff that clouds and fogs the bridge so that we are no longer able to see or walk on it.

I saw for the first time that bridge and was allowed to partly walk on it. My feet were not as steady as they should have been. There was nothing really to hold onto. Just my feet planted there for stability. To walk the Canku Luta is hard and full of obstacles but we as a people must hold onto that road. Without a strong foothold to the Great Spirit we as a people will fall faster than anyone.

We seem to think we corner the market on spirituality and know how to get from here to there. I have seen too many fool themselves and others right along with them. Too many of my brothers and sisters seem to think they "know" what is going on.

With all the building and such on the land the trust relationship has been strained to the breaking point. The bridge has deteriorated to the point of collapse.

We cannot allow our trust to disappear like grains of sand on the wind. We will all be the worse for it. The animals and everything with them are expecting us not to let them down.

Time will tell.

Ego vs. Pride

◆

I want to clear up what I see and have been taught about this subject. It is sometimes a shady area that many seem to think is ego but is really pride.

Ego is an emotion that lends itself to mostly more ego-tripping and grandiose ideas. Pride is an emotion but stops short of the ego tripping and grandiose ideas.

When I do a job I do it to the best of my abilities and my work shows it when I am done. This is called pride in your work. Many I am sure know this and have experienced this for themselves. Ego steps in when someone wants constant gratification from this.

I am not opening old wounds but want to clarify my position. I am proud of who I am and what I do for anyone. I consider it an honor to help anyone in anything. This is pride. Not ego.

Guardians of the Land

◆

I took a walk among my friends today. The animals, plants, insects, oaks, pines and aspen and everything else that lives within these lands. Today was sunny with a warmth that traveled into the heart of my body and bones as well as in to my spirit. It created warmth that allowed for ease of travel. As I traveled world I saw many things going about their business as if nothing was going on about them. They had no fear of anything at the moment.

The birds chirped along with little ones trying to fly. Trying to learn their skills from their parents for the sake of their own future survival and those of their children. My eyesight was filled with the everyday activity of my fellow creatures around us.

The deer walking along and eating what green is present despite the shortage of water in the area. The water is coming more frequently now so it is helping the creatures catch up to where they must be at this point.

At times I lend a hand to get them where they need to be. Feeding who and what I can in hopes of prolonging the destruction my fellow humans have created for my brothers and sisters around me. I ignore the words of many that say if we do this or that we will only disrupt the natural cycle of things.

I find this logic so flawed I want to just slap those that speak these words of falsehood. We (humans) have disrupted so much of the natural world that we have no choice but to intervene to a point to allow survival to take place.

I have watched these lands be "managed" by people who know little about the "true" nature of the land. The essence of the land needs to survive like anything else. All plants, animals, insects and all others survive on this. Without its continued presence the land will never recover as it once was.

I sit in the sunshine soaking up its warmth, the warmth from the Great Spirit, the Creator. This planet we sit on is a living creature with many living creatures living upon it. Many say they know balance but when seen they see only a small piece of it…one slice. They look at only one piece at a time and not the whole.

The water that flows across these lands will soon be worth more than gold ever will. It will become the new "gold" rush to be seen. The abuse of these waters leading to pollution will make good water scarce, even for the animals, plants and insects…all creatures.

Despite all the grim that is occurring around this land the animals continue on their way with whatever means they can. Living and trying to learn how to survive in a world we have and continue to create for them.

Do the animals really know what the future holds for them? I think they do but they continue on in hopes things will get better. We are the guardians of the lands and we are doing a very poor job of it. When will we as people of these lands wake up to the fact that without the land we are nothing. We are but grains of sand on a desert being blown from here to there without any knowledge of where we are going.

Understanding the whole of the land is the only way to ensure our survival as well as the children after us for many generations to come. The land will accept you when you are ready to acknowledge your place.

Quite a few of the First Nations people have become blind to this fact due to the ever-present blindness that occurs. The constant "want" and "desire to own" things that this society thinks it needs. The land is a life giver and it can take life away just as easily.

When a person walks into the territory of the mountain lion without the proper knowledge, wisdom and respect that they deserve, trouble can ensue that this person has not taken into account. The results can be deadly…mostly for the person.

Respect for all things is the only way this world can and will survive. Earning respect from the animals and the land should be a top priority for the peoples of this land. They have to know that you will be a guardian and not an exploiter or worse yet…a murderer. There is an exchange relationship with the land and all that is on it. There is no getting around this balance. You can think in your wildest dreams that this is not the case. I will tell you this is truer than you think.

The land never hides secrets for very long. They surface with surprising speed even to this day.

The land can be as wild as you can see but there must always be a level of respect and balance within the whole circle of this land. When you step deeper into the land a whole world expands beyond ones own realm. It opens as a book and allows you to read it like a picture instead of many words that have no depth. There are many pictures to explore and feel. The land is a living, breathing mother that supports all that she gives birth to.

Once a birth has taken place made she takes the responsibility of making sure it grows strong, as it should be. A variety of tests are setup to make it strong. Without these tests it would die very quickly. Strength is the major attribute of the brothers and sisters of the land. It is not the strength that abuses or takes control and says, "I am the lord here so all must bow to me." It is a strength that helps to hold all things together has the wisdom to know what is right and treats all things with the proper respect it is due to them. No matter how small they may be. We cannot interfere with the will of Mother Earth.

This society seems to think that it should interfere at all bends instead of letting things maintain their balance. Morals and emotions have nothing to do with the survival of the land and the living creatures upon it. It all deals with balance and the maintenance of that balance.

Once the heart of a land becomes destabilized and broken it will die. It will take a long time for that area to return to its normal ways…. if it ever does. The heart of the land, as I mentioned before, is something that is unseen but still very much alive and present. The feel of an old growth forest is different from a new one with very new trees in it. It is this feel that expands to all creatures on the land. Once the "experience" and "older life" becomes destroyed, the land is different from how it was before. It is like when a company would fire all it's older employees in favor of the young ones with no experience because they are cheaper to employ. These younger employees know little of the revelations and hard spots that occur and only can experience take you through these hard times. Nothing…I mean nothing replaces experience in anything we do.

The same occurs on Mother Earth. The experience of the land can never replace anything else. When you kill off all the older things then there is nothing there to teach the younger ones have to live and make them strong. The land remains intertwined together. To continue on the current path of destruction will only cause Mother Earth to fail and then the death of us all or a large portion of us. I do not think we really want to sit here and watch our lives slowly whither away when there is no food anywhere, no water to drink. All due to the cycle of water being interrupted or corrupted by other factors and leading to an acceleration of normal processes.

The land within it has a spirit that permeates all things and causes much interconnection to occur. Without this interconnection the living things within it will die. We must wake up to the world that really exists around us and not the current environmental consciousness that is here today. This kind of consciousness only leads to violence between people and not understanding. You must wake up to see. Most people are clueless to what is really happening around them. They walk from here to there with little cares and worries.

White Road

♦

When we walk a path we walk from point to point. Whether it is red, white, black or whatever. Solving problems as we go. Each path follows like all things in life a pattern due to our events of the past. Some of those events are good and fulfilling others are bad and we would rather forget we even had them.

The Red Path is appealing to many people due to its simplicity and closeness to the Creator. When we follow our true path and not one of money, greed, vanity and many others then there is a simpler life that is lead. If one comes to a path that is not of their color should that person be told to go back to their original path? To see if it is right for them and then come back? They would not be here if that path was correct for them…. Hmmm, this is a hard question to answer especially when we have not seen the path that they left? What guided them to this time and to this path?

Many have walked this white road and are very dissatisfied with this way. Do we have the total right to say, "This is our path? You have no rights here. Go back to your path and find wisdom there first before you come to ours." I believe we do not have the "exclusive right" to tell someone this. The Creator is one to all no matter what color, ways, background, ect. They may be.

What I have found is that we as a people are becoming as prejudice against others as we are against our brothers and sisters. Why? The more one fights a wall the more it does not move. It becomes harder out of defiance. Wisdom and education are what's needed. People are here for a reason. They have come here to learn why we are how we are and try to make their lives more simple and honorable. As we go down our path as a people we are losing our own sights because of all the side tracking. I maintain my way no matter what society says. No matter who crosses my path.

No two paths can ever be mixed. Ever. This causes great confusion within our lives. All paths cross at some point for it is inevitable. When we speak of asking someone to follow his or her own path what decision are we making? Are we not practicing a small part of bigotry? You stay over there and I will stay over here! We are not right for you or you for us. No one can make this decision for some one else. It seems I learned somewhere that we cannot tell another how or what to do with their life. Has this been forgotten?

It seems it has been.

Why There Are Trees

---◆---

Here is a story I tell my kids when we walk through the forest.

Why there are trees.

As a tree grows from it beginnings as a seed it does not really know where it will be or where the wind will carry it. It finally settles somewhere where the Great Spirit has placed it. It gains nurturing from the sun, soil, water and all other things around it.

The leaves of the other trees that have grown strong and wise will shade and protect it. It's also shaded by others who always try to reach to the sky as fast as they can. Eventually it will end up leaning on their neighbors for support. As the tree grows, it spreads its roots out under the ground to provide support for it to grow and get its food. When you reach for the light of the sun you gain air to breathe and give back that which all living creatures need to survive. Within that tree there are individual pieces that work together to support and give life to the tree.

When it storms the leaves become exposed but attached to those that know it needs the leaves to survive. It also knows that when a leaf gets too big for itself it will end up coming off and dying. Only to be replaced by another in its place or somewhere close by the original spot. As you work your way down, the small little veins or tunnels carry its life throughout it and give it life giving food to all no matter where they are on that tree. They know nothing of who gets it...good or bad. They still get it.

The outside covering protects all those inside so that the tree maintains it health as best as it can. As we move into the roots we see many individual pieces together trying to get the water and food into the tree so that it can stay healthy. When the soil and air surrounding the tree become polluted with whatever is there the tree tries to fight it off as best as it can. It becomes limited for it only knows what it knows. The individual pieces try to stave off this pollution by trying to adjust it self in anyway it can. Despite all this internal adjusting going on the outside still strives for the sun and its sunlight. Ever reaching for it. It grows and grows despite the pollution it absorbs from all around it. Despite the storms that rage all around it the pieces always seem to hold it to the ground.

When the roots become shallow it is when the tree meets it greatest test of strength and endurance. It may have covered itself by spreading its roots over a wide area but the depth is not there. The strength in deep is not there. It is usually when a stronger than usual storm comes along does it meet its match. It falls the ground with a crash heard all around. Despite this tree perseverance and wanting to overtake all around it forgot

About how to be strong and hold steady no matter what comes along. It forgot how to dig its roots deeper to hold for greater strength. It forgot that being bigger is not necessarily better. The oak tree grows slowly and deeply as it reaches for the sunlight. Its components reacting to the environment but still making sure it roots grow ever deeper and stronger so that the rest of the tree can remain strong. Live life to learn and bend in the storms. To grow the roots ever deeper so that when the storm tries to blow you over you stand with strength. No tree is perfect but to forget that it needs all its components to remain strong and healthy is foolish.

Remember the tree for it speaks of life and all that need its wisdom. It supports and gives shelter and food to the many creatures around it.

It gives to those that are not even anywhere close to it. It still works in conjunction with all. If a tree stands alone it will not stand for long. Listen for it speaks loud to those that are silent.

Between Sight and Sound

———————◆———————

I have had the opportunity to take walks and listen to people. Within the confines that I had I did see and hear many things. Things that are there but wondered if anyone every looked hard enough to see and hear these things.

If you have sight then try to see what I am trying to say. When you hear something in the woods do you exactly know what it is? Or are you assuming you know? Acting like a big shot and guessing so that others think you are up on the aspects of the woods. The woods with all its sights and sounds. The woods with even all of its emotions.

Within a forest or land there lays its emotions. So many I find it tough to sort out at times. All the emotions from Mother Earth, the creatures and from the Great Spirit. It lies between the sight and the sound. I thought it was a separate part from it but it is within a particular place. When watching things all around you and without the ability to do much makes you sensitive to it. The emotions of animals are a unique thing to watch, see and feel. We all think "Aw what a poor unfortunate thing."

Well, hey, at one time they were thinking like that about us. Such a strange thing to have the tables finally turning and now we turn our backs on that which keeps us alive. The emotions of nature between the sight and sound need to be heard so they will not be lost. They cry out for our help and justice. Hmmm....Such similarities we share with our brothers and sisters here on turtle island and mother earth. Think about it.

What is "Medicine?"

---◆---

Many have tried to say what medicine is. What is "good" medicine and what is "bad" medicine? Many don't know what it "really" is. They have not been taught the difference between these and what constitutes either one of these. "Good" medicine is that which flows for the good of a person or a people. "Bad" medicine is what flows that creates or wreaks havoc on a person or a people.

Sacred objects have either good medicine or bad medicine. They can allow good or bad medicine to flow. These objects become a symbol that allows either to flow for the good or bad of a person or a people. The objects can hold this medicine after a time and become a manifestation of that good or bad medicine.

An object then becomes a portal for either one. "Good" medicine allows that which we call good spirit to flow and enter. It allows good spirit to flow out and do things for us. It can also allow bad spirit to enter and flow.

This subject is not talked about much among our people because of the nature of it. It speaks of things that are not of this world but yet are. They pass by with little knowledge or thought from anyone.

Good medicine is what is used to help people. It heals, saves, and creates things for our well being. To help our existence for the better. There are no boundaries to this. No colors, no socioeconomic classes that are created, no religious affiliations, nothing. It flows from the Creator through the object to the destination it was asked to go…if that destination is worthy of it.

Bad medicine on the other hand creates or wreaks havoc on the person or people it was sent to. An object can hold bad medicine. It can lie there and seem to do nothing but the medicine that it holds can do what it was placed there to do. Many people use bad medicine against people. Try to use it to gain revenge, have someone go crazy (out of their mind), just do things to prove a point, or just anything that will create havoc in someone's life.

Bad medicine must be watched and carefully. To allow it to run rampant without the known consequences can be devastating not only for the person or you. Most of the time these are quite recognizable by those that know of what they are. There are others that seem to think they know how to handle either one. Think again.

Only an experienced person knows how to handle these and handle them correctly. You must do your best to remember this and stay away from those that claim they know how to use them. A wicasa/winyan wakan knows but very few outside of this circle do.

Respect

———————— ◆ ————————

What is respect to you? Do you really know what it is? Are you able to give respect without the emotions or intellectual garbage twisting it to your viewpoint? There is little respect for anything nowadays. It seems to be a passing fancy, even among native people. The things that need to be taught are not. Intolerance for things seems to be a path people are taking now. "My path is correct and the true way so others can take a hike." A rather erroneous thought at that. This reminds me of how politicians treat people, with little to no respect unless there is something attached to further "their" cause. The treat people more like cattle to be played with and a source of income for their pockets.

Respect is earned. It is not something like, "Here I am respect me!" It seems people "want" to be respected for what they do. They do something good or great and they "expect" respect.

Among our people respect is given to those that have "earned" that right. There is a basic respect for all but there is a deeper respect for those that fight for our people in battles, help the elderly and the less fortunate, the old ones of the nation, the elders of the people, a position that is earned within the nation, and many other reasons. It is not just something that is flaunted away at will.

Respect has been lost due to the incessant desire to acquire material things. How does one earn respect and give it in return?

Here is a story I was taught that helps to teach and helps to understand respect.

One day there was young rabbit that was hopping through the meadow on his way to find food. It was a bright sunny day without a cloud in the sky. He was hopping along without a care in the world when he came up on an older prairie dog.

The prairie dog was sitting beside his hole, as he usually does, scanning the prairie for any signs of a coyote, hawk or any other creature that would eat him. Now, this rabbit was still young in his years and still had much to learn regarding the ways the land and all that live there. He was quite inexperienced in crossing these prairies.

The prairie dog seeing this inexperience just sat and watched as the rabbit hopped by on his way to somewhere he didn't know. He wanted to ask where the rabbit was going but didn't want to interfere with his journey that he was concentrating on. The prairie dog knew that once you alter another's way that you become responsible for it. This was not an easy lesson to learn for he knew this lesson well.

He had given directions to another prairie dog friend and family as to where a good place would be to build a home and find food. He had been so proud of himself of his knowledge that he had acquired while walking these rolling hills.

A while back he ran into his friends as they were walking by on their way to an unknown destination. Instead of waiting for them to ask for directions or advice he decided to offer it without their permission. He asked where they were going and said that there was a good place over the next two hills next to a bush that was there, one of only a few on this plain. Since he was a friend they took his advice and continued on in the altered direction the prairie dog had given them.

He was quite proud of himself and his newfound knowledge. Since he had been around these parts he knew, or he thought he knew, quite a bit.

The family went over the hill and disappeared. He sat there on his hind legs very much proud of himself. He had done good he thought. Later on he decided to go see them and see how their new home was doing. He scampered along staying low and still when movement was sensed nearby.

He saw the bush from the top of the hill. He scampered even faster to get there in anticipation of meeting his friends. As he got closer he sensed something he had not sensed before. Something was wrong and he couldn't tell what yet. As he got closer his senses now grew with a strong sense of fear. He thought to him, "why should I be fearful. These are my friends."

As he approached the hill and bush with caution he noticed that his friends didn't come out to greet him. To him this was also unusual to see. The sense of danger he couldn't seem to shake. Something was here that he had not felt before. He was totally unaware of this. As he came to the bush he saw something that he thought he would never see. His friends lay dead along side of the hill not quite to the bush.

This confused him. He thought this would a safe place for them to live and keep their family. He soon found out that on theses prairies live snakes.

The Coyote Walks Among Us

◆

I sit here tonight watching a tape that was gotten and played. Within this story was a feeling of anger and pain. This story brought feelings up from their source that I have felt for so long that I cannot remember.

It was the story that angered me. It made me feel deep feelings of contempt. Contempt for those that have killed my people, the women, the children and the old ones.

I have never been able to shake those feelings. The feelings of betrayal, feelings of deceit, feelings of anger, feelings that never will die until our people know and are able to move around like the wind.

The lies that still continuing today as we try to keep the sovereignty of our people. We sit and watch our TV's and listen to the music boxes that play all over. Where is the power in all of this? Where is your power in the world of the Great Spirit? Do you even have any?

Such foolish notions in all this techno crap. The spirits call for us to feel them again but who listens to them? Who listens to their whispers and power that once was?

There is no power in casinos, cars, TV's, or any of this foolish materialism. I sit here listening to the ancestors and the power they once had power within themselves and within each of the nations.

Maybe I am wrong for feeling this way but I will not succumb to the ways that will lead me or my children down this road. They will honor those that are around them, their ancestors, the elders, the old ones, their brothers and sisters. They will keep their power within themselves and grow with it. The good medicine will come out and will fight the bad medicine.

They will not succumb to the coyote and his tricks. The will run with the buffalo and ride with their courageous mounts. They will feel and listen to the wind flow. They will learn to move as it does. They will not give into this bad medicine that flows among our people.

I will never give in to it…ever. Sit comfortably and watch as the coyote enters your homes and blinds you with what it wants to. You will believe it for you will not be able to see until the blanket is finally pulled. Then what will you do. Fight then?

Listen or remain deaf for the ancestors speak their words. The trickster is alive and well so watch and listen for he may already be sitting beside you.

Within The Calm of the Wind

◆

Tonight I sat here outside while a storm was about to roll through. The storm circled as it sometimes does among the mountains in a horseshoe effect before me. The flow here is interrupted by the ups and downs of these high slopes.

I could hear and feel the lightning strikes as they occur around the land. The rain has been coming regularly now but this storm has a different character to it. It was not like most storms that pass through these lands.

The storm grew in intensity as it came across the mountains. The mountains started trapping some clouds while others traveled and grew in size rather quickly. The wind blew and it blew hard at times but it blew in a different way this time. It was moving around my body instead of trying to knock me over. It was almost like a caressing going on...a weird sort of feeling. I stood there asking to know more of why this wind did this. I closed my eyes to feel the wind and see the form that it took this night.

It was not a hard wind but a gentle one even though its gusts blew a lot of things over. It only caressed its way around me...rather smoothly. Without edges as it usually has. "Why," I said to myself, "does this feel so different from this approaching storm?"

I felt it wrap around me and talk as it moved quickly through the trees and valleys. I became lightheaded quickly because of this but continued to keep my eyes closed. Not really knowing what I might see if I opened them.

There was no fear there.... nothing. Only a calm that was peaceful. The wind was strong tonight but ever so smooth and peaceful. I thought this as a contradiction in feelings but refused to take my mind off what I was feeling.

The lightning approached very quickly as I heard it travel through the sky with a crackling like plastic scrunched together but at an intensity 50,000 times louder with a exploding noise at the end.

The wind was still gentle through all of this. I started back towards the house as the cracks came ever so close. It is not wise to stand at the top of a mountain and act like a lightning rod for them. I am attracted to their beauty at times but don't have the desire to kiss one.

Throughout all this the wind continued to be gentle to me. Its movement around my body is like the gracefulness of an eagle or hawk on the wind as it glides on its waves. I am still wondering why such a gentle wind occurred tonight for it never does with the intensity of these kinds of storms.

The gentleness within the calm of a wind is a bit unusual but I never argue with what is. Someone or something was there guiding that wind tonight that I could feel but who was would not show themselves. They only wanted me to feel who they were, not see them for it may not be time yet for this.

Patiently I will wait for another day when who or whatever was there that produced that calm within the wind reveals itself and allows me to see who was guiding such a gentle wind.

As I walked inside the house a rather strange thing occurred. A lightning bolt struck very close to here but just before it did the phone chirped a ring...a very short ring. First the chirped ring then the strike of the Lightning bolt. Rather interesting phenomena.

The Path of the Spirits, The Path of the Past

◆

I took a ride to an area today where the red rocks shoot towards the sky. Their size was just enough to make me feel insignificant to the world they live in. They rise above the ground like spires pointing the way to the spirit lands.

It felt good to walk among them thinking about the state of our people as well as others I am thinking long about. Whenever I become clouded at times, too much to see the path before me, I walk among these rocks, among the plant nation, the four leggeds and many other creatures of this land. Meanwhile the sun shined brightly in the western sky warming the outside of me as I walk.

The stress of today and all its seemingly endless barrage of useless noise and chatter was nowhere around me as I walked this land. I was walking slowly and feeling its power surge through me like the sun through the universe.

This walk I take, I take for all whom I know. I pray among these rocks in the quiet of the day. Sending prayers of health, happiness, peace and the lessening of pain for all. The trees sit quietly listening to my thoughts. They reach their branches over to shade me from the sun. Today the path I am walking lies quiet and calm.

I walk quietly so as not to stir the spirits of this land. It is these spirits that help me from time to time and they need their rest like all else does. They stretch their arms to greet me when the toughness of the path wears me down. Their quiet manner calms my nerves while the land holds me close for today it is needed for the many things I carry.

These spirits gladly help and I hold my thoughts very close for they have walked this path before me and know where I stand. The spirits of the trees and plants come forward to touch my spirit. They grasp the things that bear so much weight for me today.

The ancestors that walked this land walked before me with pride. For they know the path that is before me and knows where it leads our clan. I pray to the ancestors and spirits of this land for today I walk their path. The path of the spirits, the path of the past, the path for which I have come to bear. This path is hard for I must carry it with pride. The ancestors are watching and hoping that I will not fail them now.

Within these rocks the ancestors have walked. I hope that I will walk as many have walked this path before me. I will carry what I need to do for it is these spirits I see, I feel that I pray among these rocks today. I stand for the ancestors and all that they have beared so that their lives will never be in vain.

The Unspoken Words

♦

Today I sat and listened. Listened to the birds. Listened to the insects. Listened to the wind. Most of all, tonight I listened to a dear friend. A friend, whom despite the long miles, I have grown to respect for her insights and words.

Even as we spoke there was a closeness of respect. Many seem to think distance causes friendships to die but I always tend to differ. If you really want it to grow it will and no amount of distance will separate that friendship.

As we talked the warmth of the heart began to emerge. Friendship can never be separated regardless of what is involved.

Tonight a rather interesting thing happened again. The first time I thought was coincidence but tonight made me a bit uncomfortable at first. It involved a sapling of an oak tree.

Tonight I was watering the plants so they would get the water they needed to survive this dryness we have here. I was watering all the plants that I could so they wouldn't shrink up and die. When I got to this particular sapling it did again what it did about a week ago.

As I watered the sapling it very slowly bent over so that it was at about eye level to me. At first I stood there looking at this wondering what was happening. I was getting a little nervous at the same time. No other tree or sapling did this so why this one?

At that point a strong feeling came over. I am not quite versed in the tree language despite all my years in the forest but this sapling was definitely trying to say something. The feeling was strong enough to get some kind of point across. The point that I was feeling but could not quite hear was that it was thanking me for watering it and was grateful for it.

I thought to myself, "I thought I have seen everything." There is always something that keeps you on your toes and rethinking about the world around you. I started to think of the significance of both, our talk and this tree.

Both are similar but yet in two different worlds. Both I belong to and both I have respect for.

Both grandfather and father would always say, "if only trees could talk, the stories they would tell." after that statement they would give a smile that you knew there was something behind it. Something that they knew was there.

Trees do in fact talk and listen as well. Maybe both my friend and the tree shared the same feelings. Both were bending an ear to listen and both were grateful for the friendship. This is only my observation on life itself. A continual learning experience. But yet maybe the sun has fried my brain a bit and is creating hallucinations. Maybe it was just the unspoken words that we all share together but never really speak about. Either way it really doesn't matter for both I respect and both will always remain close to the heart

Walk Among The Oaks

◆

I took the kids out today on a walk to pick acorns for acorn bread. They were very inquisitive regarding these small nuts off the trees. There were many shades of brown and green present for them to see. Some of the acorns were small, some were large. Still they stood there looking at them.

As we walked through the trees they began seeing them in various stages of life. I explained to them that trees are families too. They have youngsters, newly born, middle age and the old ones.

All these trees are related in some way to each other. The first tree grew and then produced others around it. Those trees had seeds that spread and the newly born grew into youngsters. The youngsters grew into adults. They then grow into middle age. Later they grew into the old ones that have gained a lot of experience in the elements and the land around them.

They had many experiences valuable to the existence of the rest, which helped the younger ones survive. The older ones passing on their knowledge of life to the little ones so they may grow strong in their wisdom and power.

The acorn like any other seed, growing from newly born to an old one if the Creator allows it to be so. Each tree and plant on its own path learning from environment around it. Learning many things from many ways it sees things.

There is communication amongst these trees for you feel it as you walk through. It feels good to walk through for some of these trees. They have been here much longer than I have been on this land.

As we walked we saw many other kinds of trees, shrubs and plants. I explained that they too also have the same family history on this land and that their contribution was just as important as all the other plants around. No one plant or tree was less important that the other. All have a part to play.

We continued on through the Plant Nation with all its varying families within it. Teaching about each and why we use them. The reasons for the various berries that grow and the need to preserve these for our winged friends that helps with their survival. Not picking everything and leaving for others to eat.

Their point of view changing a bit on how they see this world around them. A combination of many nations getting along with each other in order to survive. All the nations balancing together to help create balance within our own nation. Teaching them the need to balance what they can within the lives they lead. Without the Plant Nation nothing would be here and neither would we.

It is difficult for them to comprehend all that I am saying to them. Some of it they understand, others will come in time. The need for them to understand about this land we live on. The need to maintain that balance and understand that balance. The need to understand what we "really" need and what to leave

Behind so that others may eat and survive.

The land is there for them to understand. The land wants them to understand. It is more than willing to teach so that peace can reign with the land and not the constant turmoil and destruction of today. What we claim to be "progress."

The future of these trees and the rest of the Plant Nation are dependent on their knowledge and understanding of it. This small walk through will teach them much, and so much more to come.

The teaching of any tree, the Plant Nation and the land teaches us much.

Listening is the only requirement.

The Limit of Infinity

---◆---

Over the past few months changing has occurred at such a rapid rate that I wonder if I will have enough energy to make the trip. This trip has gone deep into the direction of the west. Deep into what I thought I knew but yet knew little to the expansiveness of it. I have traveled to areas I thought never existed within our boundaries of life.

The West teaches many things in many ways and not just from areas of what people think exist. This area is like a forest without light at times. Like traveling through a blackened forest at night. The darkness can be overwhelming and yet teach many things that you might think are frightful.

The power present in this direction is known only by the limit of infinity. Dreams come from this direction that encompass many aspects of life and continue to influence every part. Traveling through ones dreams can become hazardous and a complete testing of the will, not only in dreams but also in life itself.

We really work in all directions at once but depending on the situation only certain strengths...or weaknesses...come forward. It is sometimes difficult to face these because we show that we are weak. But if you don't see your weaknesses then how do you work on them...in silence?

The West is a vast area of unknown territory that can leave you weak and devastated when facing certain things within your life. The ability to stick to your thoughts and path become tested at every turn.... at times without end and without compassion. Its path can lead you anywhere and everywhere that you may not want to be or go. Within the darkness there lies a sliver of light that you hang onto so that the darkness doesn't consume you.

You travel through this darkness in hopes of finding its end. You pray to the Creator for guidance through this part in order to get to the end of it only to see another circle right after it. You gasp at the continual sight of circles interweaving themselves throughout the life you are leading right now. Finishing one circle to move onto the next.

The dream world interlaces here and moving almost at times in a backward motion. But that is sometimes how it moves. It sometimes must drive you back in order to move you forward. Here in the west lay many other things related to respect and commitment. Many areas of respect there are here. All different from each other but teaching the same thread within the fabric.

Commitment is an area that seems to be a failing among many of our people. They think they have a handle on this but when you walk through this area you are tested in all areas in order to see if you will move onto the next circle.... whether it be back or forward.

I have wandered through so many areas within a very short period of time that I still wonder if I have truly made it through it. Maybe I have just hit a resting place before I walk farther on this path.... the calm before the storm so to speak. It is like walking through a very sacred area and seeing that every step you take has a meaning. and within that meaning there are more.

It seems that exhaustion wants to over take you but somehow you gather enough energy to move on...move on to another circle. Within any direction you travel so many lessons must be learned to balance yourself. Within mother earth there are these same lessons but different slightly due to the interaction of all the creatures.

This area…the west…a wondrous place but at the same time ever so dangerous for once you get caught in the web that can lurk there for a long time it can hold you. As you travel through you learn also how to manage power in the balance of things. How to maintain that balance and still be able to retain the power the west holds.

There has been much reflection and testing going on and I wonder if the journey will succeed. But that is one of the lessons here to be…. perseverance. A rather easy word to say but a rather difficult path to follow and remain on. Strength is born out of this and is not an overnight thing…a rather lifetime event I would say.

The limit of infinity is never there for when you finish one there is another to follow. It is a continual cycle of circles to follow. Each has a beginning and an end. It is just what is in between there that I sometimes wonder about.

The Path of
the Future Lies in the Past

◆

Many have said that the old ways are too "old" for our ways here is the present. They say it does not work nowadays. It has nothing to do with today and how our people will walk in the future.

This I beg to differ with them. Without the past there would be no present nor would there be any future. If it were not for the ancestors there would be none of us in the present. There would be no one for the future as well.

So why does this statement people seem to fell is so distant from them? There is too much techno involvement. There are too many plastic things in life that make our present and future on the verge of being plastic.

We sit and watch words fly by us like birds flying on the wind but no one sits and watches what those birds do. Sitting down and talking with our winged friends offers a ride to the local loony bin.

Many say sitting and doing nothing leads us down the road of complacency and laziness. We must instead run around like chickens running from the slaughter. The need to sit and allow things to pass by is a lost art.

Many call it procrastination. I like to call it "resting time with eyes, ears and heart seeing and listening." A time to sit and rest and allow the mind and body to slow down and see what is truly in front of you. Without this time there is no way of looking deep enough for the heart, eyes and ears to gain a focus.

Our children are being driven to strive for things that may at some time prove to be their detriment if not balanced correctly. They strive for monetary gains, recognition, position or anything else that creates a plastic image.

The basics are being lost faster each day and no one wants to pick up the road where others have left it in the past. Kind of like a dead-end street.

The present is strictly a worktable in which to take the things from the past and learn about them. You take these things and walk towards the future in hopes that you will learn from what the past has taught you. The ancestors know much and have much to teach if stopping for a moment is allowable in people's lives.

In many ways this fails for people because they lose sight of the past and the hand that holds them to it becomes no longer able to keep a grip. They separate and the past slips away and the future becomes jeopardized.

Blindness sets in. The coyote and spider set out to make you a part of them. The coyote with his tricks and the spider weaves it web of deceit about you and those around you.

Without the knowledge of the ways of the past and the "true" ways they are to be practiced, there is little hope for the future to remain intact. Many say they "know" how to visit the past and learn its ways. This also cannot be farther from the truth. They know little about how to link to the past and reattach people to this lost information.

These people need to sit and listen to what the spirits and the Great Spirit have to say. They need to stop trying to impress those with what little knowledge they have. Balance is being lost when reattaching the past, present and future together.

These phony people or as they call themselves "medicine men out to teach the world" are phony in themselves and lay the groundwork for the spider. No "true" medicine man would teach the world anything. The world does not listen.

All things are done on an individual basis in order for the proper reattachment to the past to take place. As usual money comes first and responsibility comes last.

There is no guarantee there will be the blessing of seeing the ancestors when you cross over and travel the path to the spirit world. One must watch, as there is deceit both in and out of the native world regarding this.

The future lies only in the past. Without the working knowledge within the present the future is like walking in a forest with dense fog. Time will tell the story of all. This has been since our people walked this land.

Decision Making

◆

I sit here tonight thinking of the things that have happened in the past. Things that cannot be changed but the pain and visions remain. We look through that pain to see how our world has changed or not changed.

Sitting here remembering the childhood memories. Remembering the memories of those I have been around. Watching how people reacted to the ways of others. Watching with an interest as to why they did what they did.

We all have seen injustices within our lives at some point. Injustices that should never have been but because of lack of insight occurred anyway. We sit and wonder why the Great Spirit has allowed this to happen. Allowed such injustices to occur. Why we say. Why.

We make decisions in our lives on what we see at the moment. What we have experienced and believe to be true. We make that decision on the basis and hope that we have done what we believe to be true.

As I walked along the tree line that borders this land I wondered what the ancestors thought as the people wanting our land were trampling them. Grabbing huge tracts of land for their own. Using the government and politicians to keep the land that was taken without permission from the ones that lived there.

What the children saw and felt. What were they to believe of all of this? Did they even have a clue as to what was happening? Many council fires burned to speak of the advancement within our lands. Fear started to increase as the advancement continued on a frightening course.

I sit here listening to those fires of ours. I listen to the talk by the children of their fears and the dreams that they have. The old ones wondering what will happen to them, their culture, their lifestyle for they are no longer youthful in their age. What will happen to our future and our land? The children wondering if the future is even present anymore or even beyond this moment, beyond this day.

The lands being overtaken like a swarm of grasshoppers eating the plants while not even looking beyond themselves. Our childhood memories are based on what we see and feel within all our senses. Past, present and future.

Many do not really care what they do to another. Just another animal to push around or even kill at their pleasure. Many think as they walk on our lands that it is free for them to take without knowing what price they "really" pay for it. The "true" price of their actions.

If others seem to think that they will deal with what is at the end of their life they may be surprised when they cross over to make that walk to the Spirit World. There are many paths to the Spirit World and some are not so pleasant. The Great Spirit doesn't forget any action that we make. The Great Spirit never forgets our walk and how we walked it. What we did upon that path as we walked among and around other people and things.

No one really knows if the decisions we make today will be right or wrong. But at times I think they really do. They just pass it off as something to be dealt with later. They only know what is based on what they know at "this" moment. Matters little of what they will see in the future.

When we walk our talk and take responsibility for what we say and do, this is probably the hardest thing to do. Every word spoken must be followed to its end. Every fluctuation of the voice listened to for its sincerity and honesty. Each syllable was speaking its truth. Or untruth.

The Great Spirit watches our footsteps and sees how we will react. Watches to see what is within our hearts. Our path is our responsibility. We do what we think the Great Spirit is asking us to do. Our hearts speak their truth in hopes we will listen.

When we sit to think about what we will do, the trees, wind and other the other creatures listen for the answer. Our free will or volition the Great Spirit gives us is a gift. A gift that weighs heavy into responsibility for us, our family and all the other creatures on our land.

Many blow this off as some old time ritualistic foolishness. To think as we walk and follow what we say and feel. I hope that I can listen to the Creator and follow my heart as it speaks its truth. We must listen for its fluctuations and hear the syllables with clarity.

The connection of volition and responsibility can never be broken. We can step aside to take a break and rest but we cannot allow ourselves to walk the path that will lead us to our own destruction. We choose our own path. Whether they are right or wrong. How it affects others around us will be our responsibility.

The Fire

---◆---

Within this life there are complexities that defy the use of logic anymore. The struggles lead one to think that the path has hit a fork in the road. What should be and what will be.

These struggles we share and try to overcome seem at times just another diversion from the road we should be on. The road map needed to circumvent the obstacles has many potholes in the road. Some big, some small and some almost non-existent but there eventually to grow as we run over them.

I am sitting here looking out on the sunset on the mountains that are walking its way into the fall solstice. The sun is setting with a brilliance that is warming and comforting. One thing I can gauge is that sun will be rising in the morning. I cannot say that with regards to this road we are taking.

On this road I am walking along the side watching all these people and things go by. Sometimes they go by so fast that it appears I am standing still. I am there wondering if anyone will slow down long enough to see what is on the side of the road. The scenery sits there in its beauty and quietness.

There has been so much talk of things to come, things to accomplish to be who and what we are, things that are minute in the whole of things on Turtle Island. We are good talkers and know what we should do but should we really do it?

Freedom and independence does not come from some ink placed on a paper for all to see. It comes from us, ourselves. Something the Great Spirit gave us upon breathing into this world.

We are becoming as complicated as the society that we are trying not to become. We are striving so hard to be on our own that we are becoming just as dependent as society has become. Some say hogwash. Stand back and look. Stand on the side of the road and watch all of that go by.

We have hit a detour that is taking us away from the road where we should be on. We are building roads to nowhere with a dead end. We are so busy fighting in the courts where the Great Spirit doesn't even exist and we are basing our lives on this.

Maybe I have lost the road somewhere but I think there is a need for us to reground ourselves and see if this road we are on is the right road. Only the Great Spirit can show you the road, not some court that knows little to nothing about anything and brags it is doing something. It is like hitting one of those potholes and really feeling the effects as it rattles your car and brain.

All of this reminds me of a massive interchange system that actually leads to nowhere. Just a constant turning off one exit to get on to another while looking up and seeing your on the wrong one and trying to get over to the one where you should be. There are so many levels, diversions and lane changes.

I stand there and wonder just what the h**l we are creating. My mouth is open like one of those massive potholes that are on that road. I think I am too much from the old school to comprehend all this massive amount of intersections, stop signs and turning onto other roads.

I think I am going to light a fire on the side of that there road and talk about the good times. Talk about the children and the laughter they bring. Warm myself by that fire and wait to see if anyone stops to share a story and smoke the pipe, speak of old times.

I will wait to see what happens. I will smoke my pipe. Tell my stories. Speak of good times. I will sit by that fire and listen to those flying by hoping to find what ever they are looking for down that road.

The fire will burn no matter what happens as long as I am able to do so. I hope that some road won't come through and smother this fire with all its confusion. If you drive by stop and sit a while. We will warm ourselves, talk the talk, smoke the pipe and speak of the good times.

I will sit there and wait for those willing to stop long enough to let life go for a while and let it fly by. I will sit and keep the fire burning on the side of that road. If you stop we will smoke and talk. Eat some good food and watch that fire flicker and burn. I think it will be a good fire. So stop by sometime, it will be good.

In this world there are many ways to fight and accomplish things that will be. Guns as you have seen have accomplished nothing but heartache and pain among our people. People are so proud of this techno. Marveling.

If you sit around the fire and look in its blazing core you will see things that will come to pass. You will see things of past, present and future. All present within that fire. It is not what you have, it how you use what you have that counts.

Crazy Horse and many others knew of these things and beat the cavalry many times. Some say we lost everything but I say we gained quite a bit. We just haven't seen it yet. That fire will speak of many things in many ways. It just depends on what you see and what you do with it.

We will not lose this battle for there is more there than you think. Come, sit by the fire and speak of things to come and things that were. We will see and feel the spirits speaking with us as we talk. They will teach us things that were lost over many seasons. They will speak their wisdom. They will warm our hearts as we warm our bodies around this fire.

Our minds will dance with things the white man knows little about. Our strategy will reflect what the ancestors have spoken and still speak.

Come, sit by the fire and watch the fire flicker and dance. It will speak of things for us to learn to battle our foes.

See what is truly within that fire.

Within the Change
of the Seasons

◆

Today I was walking listening to the wind on this fall day. The wind with all its calmness and coolness on it was signaling the changes soon to come. The hawk with its wings spread out gliding on the wind with little cares present at the time. Circling about me with a pleasure I long for at times.

The pleasure of watching the ground sail on by with my wings spread to their fullest. Sailing on the wind as it passes across these soft silky feathers. The feathers wiggling as the wind supports me and sings in ears. The joy of sailing on the voice of the Great Spirit.

I feel the changes happening within my own body as Mother Earth changes here. Feeling not only the good changes but the bad ones as well. The ants scurrying to all parts the finish their work before the snowfall seals their world until the spring thaws this world out.

The animals changing their fur colors and thickness to allow for warmth during the cold. Their attitudes are changing to increase their awareness during the lean times. Some will have their bodies decrease in metabolism and thoughts of hibernation will occur and slumber sets in.

The changes on the land are subtle as they are loud. The wind signals the departure from a warm and cozy world to a cold and quiet one. Our bodies are use to resting and sleeping during the coming season of winter. The fall prepares us for the coming onslaught of snow and cold.

Within all of this the Great Spirit still speaks it words of wisdom and peace. Within all of the changes a steadiness of what appears to be time slows and only the sun marches along to its journey of sunrise through to sunset. The sun still warms this land despite its coldness.

Within the change of the seasons we still feel the Great Spirit flow through just as easily. The wind flows through its journey to some destination chosen where it will meet others awaiting its whisper of words.

Listen and within the change of seasons you will hear its voice still. It will whisper its wisdom within your ears.

Journeys Within
the Change of Seasons

◆

Today I sat here wondering about the state of things gone by and those yet to come. I walked in the cool air today with no shoes on as usual because they constrict my feet. The shoes don't allow for movement very much and the cool air feels good to them.

As I look out towards the sunset I wonder about many things yet to be. I ponder on what I have learned and what I have been taught but still there is a nagging in the back of my mind. This nagging just seems to be persistent in regard to the constrictions placed by others and how I can best work around these constraints.

The wind flows freely anywhere it desires and I listen for its music and words of wisdom. The birds fly freely on top of the waves of the wind. Their flight is one of freedom and gentleness. They fly purposefully for food but other times just for fun and enjoyment.

As the sun sets I watch with a keen eye towards the West. Another day will rise. Another has set. Within the journey of the sun there are many places that are waiting. The journey itself is one of wonder for it moves, as it is its place to be.

The journey for each of us is like this. We rise in the morning and make our way through to the end of the journey. When the time sets for us, we go to sleep. In the journey of our lives we move much in the same way. We are born, live our lives and then the sun sets on our life here.

We take many journeys in our lives. Some good, some not so good. The animals are making their journey to better feeding areas. Their winter homes unless they do not migrate to some other place. The ants are finalizing their last minute preparations. The birds, some of them anyway are migrating south to warmer climates.

The ones that are staying here are finding warmer quarters to perch some they may sleep in some type of semi-warm sleep. The plants are making their journey into their quiet sleep for they will wake up in spring to a warm new sun for them.

There are many journeys being taken on this day. The coolness of the air flows gently across this face. I feel myself going into semi-hibernation for this is the time of rest. Winter is approaching and the journeys will begin. In this place sleep will occur except for those that must carry on.

In this season some will see the journey of the heart begin, for time will seem to stand still. It is within this season that the journey within the change of seasons will begin.

Is It Imagination or Is It Real

◆

Took a walk today on the unknown trails of Pike National Forest today. The cold had started to set in but luckily the sun started to peak its warm face through the dark clouds. It was a wonderful feeling of warmth as it permeated this tired body of mine. My second oldest son took a walk with me and we walked for a time.

In that time he asked many questions and I provided some answers. I gave only enough of the answer to make him pursue the question further on his own. To have find his own answers on his own with guidance from me. His questions ranged from anywhere you could think of.

As we walked through the tall pines, aspen, different lengths of tall and short grasses and scrub oak we came across old animal bones from sometime back. They were bleached white from the exposure to the sun but sat rather peaceful there. There were no signs of any struggle, not even by quiet thoughts.

Quite a few times we saw this and it made me wonder what the purpose was. Why were we crossing these many bones and places where animals have met their attackers? He asked why these bones must lay where they do.

I explained to him that bones are never to be disturbed unless there was a necessity to do so. You must then perform a ceremony and bury the bones properly. It was done mostly out of respect for the animal.

Otherwise you just sprinkle tobacco over them while saying a prayer and move on.

He did not yet fully understand the nature of this but accepted it and we walked on. I explained to him that sometimes animals meet very violent deaths. Sometimes it is not because of the necessity of food. Sometimes it is out of sport or the fun of it.

Once you get near a site where this has happened you start to feel it. It permeates your spirit like a magnet against a piece of metal. It is then something must be done to release this animal from its physical attachment or bondage and allow it to move on.

Some of what I explained he could not understand but I told him that in time it would explain itself.

He asked if people are like this too and I told him it does happen. Sometimes people do not know what has happened and they think they are still alive. You must then try and help them find their way again if are capable and able to do so.

In his mind I could see this reeling through like a rock in a glass factory so I let it go for now. After a while I could hear him behind me. I could hear him speaking but to whom I do not know. I thought it was me he was talking to since I was the only physical presence there. He stopped so I didn't bother to ask him what he wanted to say.

He picked up an old stick and used it as a walking stick. We moved through the forest with a quietness I liked for it didn't disturb even the chipmunks that walked nearby. We climbed to the top of the hill and headed for the car.

I asked him later why he mumbled but didn't speak up and he replied, "just talking to old bones, that's all." I looked at him for a moment and he showed a smile. Within that smile I recognized he really saw what I was speaking about but just could not explain it to me. The ability of a child to speak to things he knows little about and understands just as much. But this was different. To him it was like talking to me, made no difference.

Within that moment I realized that kids can leap across boundaries and crevasses without giving it a single thought. Then I wondered why for some reason it takes adults so long to "see" things.

The mind of a child is open and without prejudices. Their hearts are open to things we struggle with. It was so easy for them. Like a walk across a crack in the sidewalk. It is so difficult at times for adults.

He saw what I was speaking and spoke immediately to it and without thinking about it. The walk spoke of many things. The main thing he picked up was like his walking stick. Without difficulty.

Is it imagination or is it real?

You decide.

On the Side of that Road

♦

Within this life there are complexities that defy the use of logic anymore. The struggles lead one to think that the path has hit a fork in the road. What should be and what will be.

These struggles we share and try to overcome seem at times just another diversion from the road we should be on. The road map needed to circumvent the obstacles has many potholes in the road. Some big, some small and some almost non-existent but there eventually to grow as we run over them.

I am sitting here looking out on the sunset on the mountains that are walking its way into the fall solstice. The sun is setting with a brilliance that is warming and comforting. One thing I can gauge is that sun will be rising in the morning. I cannot say that with regards to this road we are taking.

On this road I am walking along the side watching all these people and things go by. Sometimes they go by so fast that it appears I am standing still. I am there wondering if anyone will slow down long enough to see what is on the side of the road. The scenery sits there in its beauty and quietness.

There has been so much talk of things to come, things to accomplish to be who and what we are, things that are minute in the whole of things on Turtle Island. We are good talkers and know what we should do but should we really do it?

Freedom and independence does not come from some ink placed on a paper for all to see. It comes from us, ourselves. Something the Great Spirit gave us upon breathing into this world.

We are becoming as complicated as the society that we are trying not to become. We are striving so hard to be on our own that we are becoming just as dependent as society has become. Some say hogwash. Stand back and look. Stand on the side of the road and watch all of that go by.

We have hit a detour that is taking us away from the road where we should be on. We are building roads to nowhere with a dead end. We are so busy fighting in the courts where the Great Spirit doesn't even exist and we are basing our lives on this.

Maybe I have lost the road somewhere but I think there is a need for us to reground ourselves and see if this road we are on is the right road. Only the Great Spirit can show you the road, not some court that knows little to nothing about anything and brags it is doing something. It is like hitting one of those potholes and really feeling the effects as it rattles your car and brain.

All of this reminds me of a massive interchange system that actually leads to nowhere. Just a constant turning off one exit to get on to another while looking up and seeing your on the wrong one and trying to get over to the one where you should be. So many levels and so many diversions and lane changes.

I stand there and wonder just what the h**l we are creating. My mouth is open like one of those massive potholes that are on that road. I think I am too much from the old school to comprehend all this massive amount of intersections, stop signs and turning onto other roads.

I think I am going to light a fire on the side of that there road and talk about the good times. Talk about the children and the laughter they bring. Warm myself by that fire and wait to see if anyone stops to share a story and smoke the pipe, speak of old times.

I will wait to see what happens. I will smoke my pipe. Tell my stories. Speak of good times. I will sit by that fire and listen to those flying by hoping to find what ever they are looking for down that road.

The fire will burn no matter what happens as long as I am able to do so. I hope that some road won't come through and smother this fire with all its confusion. If you drive by stop and sit a while. We will warm ourselves, talk the talk, smoke the pipe and speak of the good times.

I will sit there and wait for those willing to stop long enough to let life go for a while and let it fly by. I will sit and keep the fire burning on the side of that road. If you stop we will smoke and talk. Eat some good food and watch that fire flicker and burn. I think it will be a good fire. So stop by sometime, it will be good.

Path to Advancement
or Road to Destruction?

———————————— ◆ ————————————

As I have walked many footsteps the past few days I have thought much about things. How or if they flow towards the goal of "advancement." This goal I think is a false one because we as a people seem to think if we advance in our monetary and material gains we are advancing as a whole.

For some reason I believe this is wrong on all ways. Our fascination with all this computer stuff and our advancement toward sovereign nations seems hollow.

Extremely hollow.

Within all of nature, Mother Earth there is no way of advancing oneself without some sort of balancing. Has anyone every noticed how slow everything on this land or any other goes so slow?

There is a reason for this. A very clear one. Balance is a learned and constant factor among all things that perpetuate the land. If one thing leans towards unbalancing things then it is corrected plus the other parts are corrected as well.

For some reason I still feel, and very strongly even more, that we as a people are on the wrong road. This is not the path to advancement but the road to destruction.

Many will feel this is kind of way out on a limb about to break but I don't think it is. The advancement of our people or even ourselves relies on the process of balancing ourselves and advancing when we see that we will not pull other things down while trying to "advance."

Advancement relies on the whole, never one part or just a few parts and leaves the rest behind for another day or when we get around to it. We as a people are becoming so intellectually sensitive to things that we are becoming self-centered in a lot of ways.

Educating ourselves in colleges, books and such, buying all these things with the money born from "legitimate" casinos that feed the habits and psychological weaknesses of these people only pulls us down.

I am becoming more disturbed by the actions of a lot of these so-called self-appointed speakers of the people who cause blindness in a lot of ways. They are blind themselves which leads me to think, "the blind leading the blind."

Having book knowledge has no power whatsoever. None. It is just hollow words on paper that can be burned and never seen again. Many are saying that they are doing what they think should be done. Are you really though?

Is it for the people, your family, and friends or is it hidden in some way or disguised as something for the people but causes gratification to you. An ego boost because you have done this for these people or that person.

Recently some words that were spoken some time ago have come forward that was taught some 80 years ago. These words have disturbed me in a way I have not known for some time. It brought back memories of talks and visions of my early youth.

How could someone I have had no contact with and has passed on long before I was born teach things I know right now and have known for some time? The paths are very far apart and have no connection whatsoever. The visions are ever again so vivid and real.

I think we all need to rethink our positions and ask whether what we are doing is "truly" in the "best" interest of ourselves, our People and the people around us. Maybe I am losing my grip on what is "truly real." Maybe I'm not.

You can delete this message as you wish or don't wish. When you speak to the heart of the land it speaks back. Problem is what it speaks is growing more silent as the days roll on. Soon it will remain silent in the words it should be speaking.

Instead it will only resound the voices of a people that should have been but now are a part of the problem. It will echo things we don't want to hear or see but will experience first hand.

It will be like the saying, "If we do not hold dear and keep that which will keep our children and their children's children alive for at least seven generations they will curse us for no less than forever."

Walking in Forgotten Lands

◆

Today I went for a walk that took me on a journey to the Spirit Lands. I walked where the ancestors walked. The walk took me to places that once were here on this land. The walk was good.

I walked for what seemed many paces over many areas. A walk that took me through prairies, mountains and by streams that glistened with the rays of the sun. Through forests of green, past old friends of deer, elk, bear and wolves. All was there as they should be. The buffalo walking among the prairie in a sea of grass like no other I have seen.

The walk was a peaceful one and not with pretenses and falsehoods clouding my vision. There was nothing to make this vision ugly in any way. There was no politics here. No fighting or bickering. All peaceful and right. The land was as real as it was anywhere I have walked. The air was so fresh and clear. The water tasting like the smell of sweetgrass in the air.

I wondered if this was my imagination or of my own creation. Is it the real place where we go when we walk for the last time here on this land? When I walked for a while I came across a group of people that I had not seen before. Their clothes were of deerskin with only some beading present. Nothing elaborate at all.

They were very grateful and happy to see me even though I knew not a clue of who they were. This land seemed more real than any I have ever walked on. It was more real than the land I walked on where I lived. Where my children ran, walked and played.

This was very vivid in colors, more so than before. This land was a new one to me. Not like the others I have walked before.

I wondered what land I was walking at this time. I wondered where I was at, who I was with. I was a bit nervous but felt very welcomed upon this land. This group of people I do not know but it seems I have met them before or was with them somewhere before.

I was walking in some unknown land that I knew of but couldn't remember. This land was known but unknown to me. The people I have walked with before, sat with, ate with, was sad with and we all walked together at some point.

Still I could not pull out where I was. Could not bring the knowledge forward to see where I was. There was no time. The sun moved on its journey across the sky in its usual way. The stars were where they always were. The moon was ever so bright with its light shining on the ground in a whitish shadowy kind of way. Nothing was any different as it was.

The land so familiar but yet elusive to its place in my memory. I have walked through many lands but this one still was familiar but not. I sat on a rock that sat on the prairie in the sea of grass as it gently swayed in the wind. The wind was a warm gentle thing that caresses your body like a blanket.

Its gentleness was just as knowing and strong as usual and still spoke in this land where I was, where I was walking. I sat and wondered where I was and enjoy this land with its animals and people who walked upon it.

I sat and enjoyed all that I could. I would walk further on and enjoy the land and people who lived here. All the while still wondering what land I was walking in and who these familiar faces were. There are many memories here.

The lands of our ancestors are as large as it is great to see. There are many that say the see these lands but I wonder if they really do. Have they walked this land and learned their past history and the places our ancestors walked? Have they seen the water flow past these places where we lived and hunted?

There is much to be learned form the land on which I walk right now. It speaks with softness yet a strength that is quite familiar. It moves through me like a gentle breeze moves through a tree. The spirit of the land is strong. It has not been robbed like the land where we walk now. The good medicine resides here.

Walking among the people of the land is quite comforting. The spirits are gentle and true. Nothing do they hide from you. There is much to learn here of the respect, honor, skills for survival and many other aspects of our people. This is not some hokey poky land that people speak of in some fantasyland. This is life as it should be. The children playing their games while the fathers and grandfathers talk of things to come and what to do about it. The grandmothers were teaching their knowledge to the mothers and daughters. Teaching them what they need to know regarding ceremony, growing up and their responsibilities to their husbands, brothers and families.

This land speaks much of the People, not only of whom but also of what they are. The spirit of the people wanders through these lands. There is much here for the people to learn and hear again. Are there enough who know how to travel their way back in order to move forward? As I walk through the prairie grass I wonder about this. I wonder about how our people will make such travel and not be lost on the way. The air is crisp and the sun is bright. I will walk on and see what I have forgotten.

The "Feel" of It

---◆---

Tonight I sit here watching the Geminid meteors streak above my head. I look in amazement at their sight. This is something that is seen a little more frequently since I have moved into these mountains. The city lights don't shine so bright here. The wonder and majesty of Mother Earth and all that lives on it.

I sit here wondering about such things that occur outside this ball of enclosed air. The universe with its expanse, its light shows and spherical shapes sitting in a sea of waves supporting all of us.

I think how ludicrous the election of George Bush is and the impact it will have not only on our people, but on this land as well. I think of all the opinions I have heard regarding what he can do for people, mostly special interests who have lined his pockets in some way.

Within all of this I think about the purpose of vision quests and their abuses from those that think they know how they are to be done. What their purpose is. The continual need to find the "inner" self as many would say. Vision quests are a sacred ceremony among our people and to use it improperly brings disaster to those that participate.

Once a spot has been picked to do a vision quest it becomes hallowed ground for that person. To know where one is going and what your purpose is a very good thing to know and have. It allows you to follow what was set out for you in this life. It starts the person on their path in this life.

Society is lost today and many are trying to fill the void with false hopes and dreams for the sake of making money and supporting their family. They say it won't hurt because it really won't affect them that much. They are not Native in any way. How foolish a stance to take when you turn a person off their path onto another without the knowledge and wisdom of what is going to happen.

This society is creating zombies by the truckload at a rate that is alarming. It is bleeding over onto our people. It is like an open wound with no way of stopping the hemorrhaging. The materialistic desires of people and the need to feel important. The need to feel that they are accomplishing something. Each of us has a purpose in this life and we choose it early. The need to fulfill some ridiculous dream is foolish at best. Some are saying they are learning the old ways. How do you know they are old and not made up?

I have thought and been told about why some of the Old Ones live the way they do and is for good reason. When you are able to listen to the spirit of the land and the Creator you start to become quieter. You listen for things that others cannot hear. You see things others cannot see. This is where the "real" teaching begins.

The Creator and the spirit of the land bring you to your vision quest and answer your questions before they are asked. The animals play a part in this for they are there not only for basic survival but also for knowledge and when to use it. The vision quest comes to each person differently and varying intensity. What it teaches is also different to each person.

The children search for meaning and direction in their lives and we can point the way as long as we know where we are and what path we have taken. The direction they take depends on their past experiences, family and their connection to the Creator and the land.

Many do not take the true depth of things like this seriously. This is just one of those "myths" people talk about. This "myth" is just something out of the dark ages when we were foolish. A short glimpse into a "new age" and we are set for life. Such shortsighted hogwash. Without the "heart" that is needed to gain this knowledge there is a possibility that wandering further on this land than you already are is deepening.

Old traditions have a certain "feel" and "medicine" to them and there is no way to replicate them without this. If you do not know what this "feel" is like then the need to "try" things is out of your reach for now. Curiosity always killed the cat. So why do it?

A little bit of knowledge and a lot of stupidity is I guess the name of the game. Hmmm, sounds like many people both native and nonnative I have met. Walking around the pen showing how glossy the feathers are. Strutting like someone with a bad case of hemorrhoids.

Without the "feel" and the "medicine" to go with it you're just spinning your turkey legs.

The pleasure of seeing shooting stars and the stars that twinkle in the night with their blazing yellowish white tails. The wonders of the Creator for us to see and learn from.

A Walk Into Gentleness

◆

Today we took a walk into gentleness. The family took a walk out into this winter wonderland. The temperature is a measly 5 below and the wind blows only slightly if at all. We take the walk to listen to the ever gentleness after a large snow like this. It has snowed about a foot here.

Everything is covered. Everything as far as the eye can see. It is quite a magnificent sight to see. The Colorado Blue Spruces hold their branches high regardless of the weight they carry. The hawthorns have a small line of snow along their branches and the needles stick out ever so well. It is a continual reminder that to watch, not to run into their branches.

The blue birds, blue jays, magpies and many others fly to find food that has been a bit scarce due to man's interference in its food chain. We supplement their diet so they have a chance to survive the onslaught of so many things into their world. The snow seems to cover up all the abuse that people seem to instill on her any way they can.

The quietness of the trees in their slumber seems to be still a reminder that life renews regardless of what is still unseen. The snow blankets the grass in the fields like the waves on top of the sea. The snow is rolling along in an ever-present sea of sparkles. The sparkling was coming from the sun rising behind our heads on this cold crisp morning. Colors can be seen from different angles if one takes the time to look. The kids have fun with this but it also helps them to see things from many ways.

The air is quiet but cold. It speaks with a gentleness I enjoy on these days off. The kids enjoy these walks for they allow us time together. They are also for the teachings of the world around them in a "realistic" manner. There is nothing clouded or hidden out here. There are no hidden agendas. There is nothing that is faked, colored or seen as a false front in any way. What it is is just what it is. Nothing more, nothing less.

The animals do not treat you will ill respect. They treat you with a respect that everyone and everything deserves. They give you the distance you need to allow the young ones to grow. They also get close enough for the young ones to see them in full view and almost as if you could reach out and touch them.

The animals do allow, with time and "earned" respect, for you to come closer and touch them. They will allow you to hold their young in your arms and allow help from you to raise their young as well as your own if you allow them. They teach a wisdom and knowledge that is unmatched by anything anyone could teach. Their gentleness of spirit no matter who the four-legged, winged ones or whomever it may be.

They will allow you to feel the softness of their antlers when the fussiness is there. It is something to feel. The softness of their coats and skin. Their eyes are ever so gentle but watchful. They watch for those that would do harm or any predator, including humans, that would hunt them like they are some sort of childish game.

I live among a lot of these people who call themselves "hunters." They walk through the forest thinking these animals are in fact dumb in their manners. These "hunters" really do not have a clue of what the world around them is all about. The four-leggeds have learned over the seasons to keep a wary eye, ears and nose open for the "scent" of change and when hunting season occurs. There is a change and scent I have noticed in the air. They feel and know what is happening and move to other places where hunters can't go. Safety for their young ones and families is now a priority.

Despite all the onslaught of people, houses, pollution, deforestation, devastation and the many other ways people destroy things they come in contact with, they continue to remain gentle in their spirit and mannerisms. Even the bucks know when we are around but are not fearful for we have no need to hunt them. This they know.

The kids learn that the animals are gentle in their manner and the ways they raise their kids. They are only "scary," as the kids say, because of misinterpretations from this society and educational system. They are only "scary" when are trying to protect their lands, their clans, their families, their food and also their own lives. They, most times, don't trust anyone. They "know" who "you" are.

The gentleness of the land permeates their spirits and permeates their lives. Mother Earth can be a harsh place to live but all of the time she gives as much as she wants to you as long as you learn her balance and maintain it. A fox, to us he is known as "Freddie," in his winter colors is a wonder to watch. His coat ever changes with every season. The kids wonder at this site. They are amazed at his "how does he paint himself?" coat. I still wonder at this as many times as I have seen this is my life of all animals.

A coyote that lives on these lands scurries quickly across the grass into the nearby trees. His legs are too short for this deep of snow. Mother Earth never leaves anyone out in the cold. She always has the means for you to survive on her lands. The coyote is just as important, I tell the kids, as any animal there is. He keeps the mice and other small animals in balance so they do not overwhelm the land and the other creatures that live on her.

The kids with their curiosity tests the limits of how much I can speak in one sentence. Many questions are spoken but I only speak to say, "Sit, look and listen. All will be taught in its time and place. Only patience is needed to see what you want."

We walk back towards the house and the kids playing in the snow. They are learning to "see" the world around them and to listen so that they can hear and learn what Mother Earth wants them to learn. I teach what is needed for them to follow their hearts and respect all that there is around them. This land is for all to survive on and without respect for all the creatures, plants, stones and many other things on her there would be no balance at all.

We have walked through this world of gentleness but many would say otherwise. Hurricanes and tornadoes have an eye of gentleness that is seen within its center. Many wonder why this is so. A "strange" phenomenon of some kind scientists says. I just smile for it is only a reflection of Mother Earth herself. She may be rough on the outside but the gentleness will always be there on the inside.

All of nature is the same way. So hard they say, but really so simple.

A Walk Into Change

◆

This story was written for my children to learn on how the world can change with little notice. When we don't listen we can suffer not only as an individual but our family, friends and everyone around us suffers. The decisions we make everyday can change ours/everyone else's path forever.

A Walk into Change

There was a Lakotah man named Flows like the River who lived on the side of a river near the village where he and the People lived for the change of seasons. They came here from the time the winds grew warm and the ducks returned to the time the winds grew cold and the leaves turned to yellow. They then moved into their winter lands that helped protect them from the grueling winter winds and snows that occurred within their lands at the snow existing time.

One day he sat on the bank watching the river move by at a pace that was smooth and easy. The winter snowmelts had slowed and allowed the stream to slow its furious path to an easier one where everyone could enjoy its movement. The sun was warm and life was busy with setting things up and getting everyone where they wanted to be.

He sat there watching a colony of ants and other creatures scurrying around now there was a steady stream of warm air that warmed their places. They knew the seasons had changed and wanted to air their places. They scurried and moved in a way that amazed him. He wanted to see more so he just sat there and watched. He watched and listened to their continued journeys about their land.

After a while the leader's son, Running Fox came by. He walked and stepped on many of these creatures without any thought to what would happen afterwards. He just walked right on by and even ignored him. He gave no acknowledgement to either the creatures or him. His rather arrogant attitude was well known throughout the tiospayes and clans. He thought since his father, Walking Bear was the leader of the People he could and would do as he pleased.

Flows like the River was quite irritated at such actions and really had little respect for him. He felt there was little to be respectful to. He did so anyway for this was what he was taught. He was taught to respect all things and not disregard anything or anyone. All was a part of the Great Spirit. That to disrespect was disrespect to the Great Spirit. Running Fox walked on as if he had nothing in the world to care about.

Flows Like The River continued to watch these creatures and see how they would survive now that a lot of them were destroyed. Killed by Running Fox's disrespectful arrogance and lack of insight into the world that supports him. As Flows Like The River watched it seemed that there was nothing but chaos due to the destruction of their homes and ways.

The ants scurried even faster to understand what had happened. They searched all around for their comrades. The ground where they lived was mangled and destroyed. They scurried to find a new way to go. They moved around trying to repair their homes. Moved around like there was no rhyme or reason to his or her actions. He could almost hear their voices. Voices that were chaotic.

He had remembered many times when Walking Bear, the Leader of the People made decisions that made little sense. Those decisions not only had consequences to him but to all of the People. He remembered the times when decisions were made on arrogance and infighting and later proved to be very disastrous.

His memory was flooded with the time many seasons ago when the Council had made a decision to hold off and wait until the sun made its journey a few more times before moving camp towards the winter lands. They wanted to gather more berries, nuts and meat for the winter. They wanted to make sure that there was no doubt that no matter how severe the winter was that they would survive without a problem.

Despite the fact that Mother Earth had signaled an early winter, no one was moving. The winds started blowing cold earlier than expected. There was apprehension on his part to stay. Mother Earth was telling them to move for the winter snow was coming.

Many of the winged ones were moving. There was much activity of his brothers and sisters into their homes and places to protect themselves. He knew this was not a good decision. He approached the Council and asked them to change their decision and move the People to the winter lands. The winds, the brothers and sisters of the land were speaking of winter fast approaching. The Council refused for it was agreed that more food was needed. More was to be gathered for the winter. They thought he was a fool who lost his mind.

They paid him little mind. Running Fox even ridiculed him for his "listening" to these "things." He said that they should stay and continue gathering and ignore his ramblings. Walking Bear, Running Fox and Council didn't want to hear anymore of this man's ramblings of "listening" to the winds, creatures, four-leggeds, winged ones or any other "foolishness" he was speaking. He left the Council and walked back to his tipi. There he thought for some time what consequences would come upon the People. Now that they have ignored the signs and voices to leave this land.

He decided it was time for him to leave. He didn't care what the others thought. He could not allow the signs the four-leggeds and Mother Earth was telling him. Very few went along with him. There was concern in his heart that Walking Bear, Running Fox along with the Council had made the wrong decision. He packed up his belongings and tipi and rode towards the winter lands. He continued on his way knowing that the weather was soon to change more rapidly than he even thought.

As the sun journeyed across the sky a few more times the wind grew colder and stronger. The four-leggeds moved to their wintering grounds early. They knew better. The day's light grew shorter with less and less time to gather. After the sun journeyed a few more times the clouds came with a darkness that no one could remember. The snow came with a fury like a herd of buffalo crossing the hunting grounds beyond the trees. The place where the land seemed to go on and on without a tree in sight but there was a land of black that moved.

It snowed for so long there was no way to tell if they would be able to get out and move to the winter lands. The time now was marked only by the light and darkness. No one saw the sun or moon for some time. He was greatly concerned that decisions were made without much wisdom or listening. They were made more on arrogance and the lack of listening to the world around them.

Without the wisdom and knowledge that Mother Earth can give many problems can occur. While the People tried to gather their things, the snow and winds increased in intensity. The snow was rising faster on the ground than they thought. The tipis were hard to get out of the ground and wrap up. It was hard to see what was going on. Everything was freezing and cold to handle.

Walking Bear and the Council met to see what could be done. They knew there was enough food for a while so concern was not there to move right away. The decision was made to wait until the snow subsided and then move the village. The snow continued to fall at the same pace that it started at many days before.

After many days of light and darkness had passed, they started to become concerned. They were starting to think that maybe they had been wrong about not "listening" to Flows Like The River. They knew he had left for the winter lands. Walking Bear and the Council were concerned that maybe they should of just packed everything up and moved to the winter lands.

The winds howled and the snow fell from the clouds in the sky. There was no mercy for them it seemed. They had to do something for they couldn't stay here. The winter would be too severe and the food would not last in this land. The decision and supply were made on the winter lands.

They decided to break their homes down and try to make a path to the winter lands. The little ones were huddled into a couple of the tipis and the rest were taken down until the last minute. The horses were packed and the elders were placed on horses to make the long journey there. There were not enough horses to take everyone. The rest had to walk through the snow and take turns riding the horses. Children had to be carried as well as the packs of belongings that were supposed to be on some of the other horses.

There was no more he could think about for this was the winter where many of the People and animals died along the way. Many died because of the arrogance and ignorance of a few.

When the People finally arrived at the winter lands a new Leader and Council were appointed. No more was the decision left to a few people. The decision now rested on many. The People as a whole made the decision.

As he watched the ants and creatures move about he noticed that after a time there was some sort of order. Even though many of their numbers were killed they continued on with what was going on. From the random act of violence on these creatures he learned many lessons.

He learned that when you disrupted something on their path you change the circle as well. It can be either good or bad. When an ant or any creature is killed it must have a replacement nearby so that the disruption is not permanent. When there isn't the circle loses its strength and small problems occur.

When the smallest creatures are eliminated the circle starts to weaken. It moves onto the next thing that relies on it. If it is not there or there's not enough the next thing suffers and on and on. It goes on until the whole circle is disrupted and a rebalancing must occur.

Something that is taken away must be replaced by something else. When it is not there the creatures and Mother Earth loses its balance. As more creatures are killed the balance falls further. The circle continues until rebalance occurs, either slowly or swiftly.

When we walk our path our thoughts, deeds and general activities causes other things to change around us. These changes can be good or bad. The changes affect everyone and everything around us. No matter how minute it may be. A word, gesture or nothing done at all when it should have been, has effects on everything.

When the circle loses a piece it can regain it in time and the circle remains strong. When many pieces are lost the circle weakens and soon it must correct itself. Mother Earth will not stay out of balance for long. The signs are there if you "listen" and "hear" what she is saying.

The smallest creature speaks many things. How many can you hear?

The Native Trail of Knowledge

◆

Today I went for a walk among the red rocks today. I traveled alone but alone I know I never will be. I walked quietly so I could hear what was being spoken. The ancestors walked through these same rocks and wondered at their size as they shoot their points towards the stars. Soon the kids will be here and I will walk them through this trail of knowledge and show them where their knowledge lies.

The wisdom that is spoken not only by these rocks but also by all things that are here is timeless. The winged ones, the multitudes of little critters that crawl and fly, the four-leggeds of all sizes, the plants, trees and all the other nations that speak their words for us to learn.

I walk through here wondering what many have said and thought. I wondered on their travels through this path called the "Indian Trail" for it was the passage that many traveled to get through these mountains. This area was plentiful in animals, plants, water and shelter. It was, and still is, a way station for those that are weary in mind, heart and spirit. The spirits are here still walking this path for it is their choosing to do so. To speak words that are timeless and still passing their wisdom to those that will listen. I walk here wondering about how many of my people, and all other colors alike, act like they know what is going on.

I wonder why I still argue with the fools of our time and not just allow their words to pass on into the mist of the morning air to be destroyed by the morning sun. The words that speak without the thought of silence before them are burned off. Within the silence there is time for the proper sequence of words to be spoken if they are to be spoken at all.

The birds speak their words in a way that gives time for them to hear what they need to hear and speak what they need to speak. The animals only speak what they need to and hear what they need to as well. It seems that this entire information overload has caused many to forget who and what they are.

There is much here to listen to and hear. I see visions of my people on the prairies living among the grasses, trees, the buffalo and other four-leggeds, rocks and many other things that allow for our teachings and growth. The children learning form an early age what the world is really all about around them.

The air here is crisp and clear for once. The pollution here has gotten worse due to the increase of people and machines. The pollution hangs here now like a smoke in a room with no windows or doors to let it out. I am watching the cycle of a land once pristine in its beauty being slowly abuse and destroyed.

Many are trying to "reclaim" the land. This is something that is not possible until all machines and pollution is ceased. This land is not infinite in its capacity to reclaim itself. It can only hold so many people and so many things. It cannot support a large population and filter all the stuff it produces.

The changes we are seeing are but a glimpse into that which we will see. We will see what Mother Earth is truly capable of. Many will speak their words of some "mystical" thing that is happening and that the Natives that listen not only to the ancestors but also to the old ones are in some way "mystical" fools.

These words I find now to be nothing but foolish talk out of the mouth of fools that know little of the world around them. They know little of the "true" world our people lived in and their ways of connecting to Mother Earth and to all their creatures for their wisdom and teachings.

The ancestors that walked through this land knew of what they had to do, what they knew of their land and all that walked or lived on/in it. The land speaks much and will teach anyone who is willing to "listen."

Without the knowledge of the land the lost remain lost. There is nothing that can survive unless there is knowledge of the land and all that speaks within it. To think otherwise is a fool's stance. The land is willing and unwilling at the same time. To those that listen and "know" what is there will see what is needed for survival to take place.

The false knowledge created by this society travels through people's minds like the pollution that hangs within these lands. Without the knowledge of our ancestors and the lands they lived on nothing will survive as it once did.

The Native trail of knowledge is not found anywhere but within the lands, our old ones and our ancestors.

But in order to "listen" one must learn to "hear."

Later on the whole group was together within these of towers of stone jetting towards the sky. The kids were as anxious to see them as I was. The sun is alive in its glow of sunlight streaming towards the ground. The rays of the sun hitting us with all its warmth in the still chilly air.

Questions of how do animals know when an earthquake is coming was on their minds. The recent events of Seattle still fresh in their minds. The concern for the people, four-leggeds, winged ones and all others that live within the lands that surround it.

I explained that within time the elders of their group teach the young ones what to look for and feel when Mother Earth shakes herself. The air changes, the "feel" of the land changes and most of all Mother Earth sends out signals early enough to warn her children she is about to make a change in herself.

Most of the time the human component of these lands totally ignore these small but significant signals. When the seasons change these same kind of signals emerge. The "feel" turns into knowledge in time for a catalogue of each one is preserved for future reference when the time is needed to use them.

They laughed many times when I told them that when cockroaches come out of the woodwork and start spinning that an earthquake was soon to happen. The thought of a cockroach even being around made their skin crawl. I said, "Nonetheless all things must be looked at before you dispel their ugliness as something repulsive."

We continued on that flowers react a certain way when danger is close by or eminent. Some close up while others seem to quiver slightly when there is no wind or need to. Their "feel" is much more acute than ours and can't be discounted either.

Also just before Mother Earth shakes there is complete and utter silence. A "dead" silence that is so eerie and quiet, it is disquieting. Your inner sense is kicked into high gear when you suddenly hear this.... this "dead" calm. This occurs also before hurricanes, tornadoes and severe storms.

The four-leggeds and winged ones will move in the direction away from the center as it moves towards them. Almost as if avoiding a prey even though none are around. Their senses are increased to the point of fear in their eyes.

There are times though even they are confused when these shakes occur deep within and not near the surface. Much like an arrow coming at them from under the ground rather than along the surface where the wave precedes the actual earthquake. The wave is coming to their feet from directly underneath than far away.

This is the hardest to see and react to for anyone, animals and humans alike. I ask them to look at the creatures around them and try to "see" what they are doing and "feel" what they feel. This is not an easy task for it must be learned as you go along and practiced so that when danger is around the four-leggeds, insects, winged ones and many others can tell you where they are coming from and what direction.

I tell them that these mountains we live in were created by earth-quakes and that these lands are still "active" within their bases. They can still move at anytime and shift their feet anywhere at anytime. We are really no different than any other part where the lands collide together and shift now and again.

One should never be complacent on these lands for change is an ever-constant thing. Once you are comfortable then Mother Earth will change that. She will never allow you to remain comfortable for long stretches unless it is deserved otherwise. Only until she says so will this be so. This is her choice, not ours.

None of the plants are alive yet and the rocks stream forth their warmth. The reflection of the sun's journey travels across the very blue sky today. Our people were so sensitive to the land that they knew sometimes decades in advance what was going to happen. Sometimes very short periods, but enough time for a move to occur quickly.

What you dismiss as bogus stupidity may sometime save your life. These lands speak volumes if the eyes and ears are seeing and listening. I teach my children to step outside of preconceived notions and "see" what is going on. "Feel" what is happening and use all things around them to understand the whole picture. Without this you can become blind to an aspect that will lead you to a great many things.

Come, sit by the fire. See, listen and feel what the land has to offer you. Without it we cannot call ourselves a people anymore. We are nothing but grains of sands on a beach somewhere. Hoping that when the tide comes in we are swept into what we want. It may turn out to be nothing we care for.

Knowledge is everywhere and the trail is growing cold. The Native Trail of Knowledge is there to walk on anytime we are willing. It takes little effort once one steps here. Many have, and our ancestors knew this trail well. Once it is lost it will take much to regain.

As Mother Earth Opens Her Heart

------------------------------- ◆ -------------------------------

Today the kids and I took a walk in the warm sun and gentle cool breeze out onto the land. The land was warm despite the cold winter that comes through here. We walked through the still bare oak trees. We walked on the usual path down into the valley below but on the way we stopped many places to see Mother Earth being reborn.

The small plant nations bringing out their leaves to soak up this bright warm sun. The plant nations of all kinds is good to see and teach the kids what plants come up first and what purposes they may serve if needed sometime. They inquire about the bees that have finally come out of their homes to greet this warm gentle sun today.

Mother Earth opens herself for another year of growing that will allow these winged ones, four-leggeds and the many insects to live and continue their ways on her. Bringing their part onto this land that allows all to balance on her.

We come across a young doe the gets up off the ground and scampers with its legs about four feet of the ground. A rather intriguing and amazing sight for them to watch. They ask how she can jump so high and so fast. They stand there watching her fly quietly on the wind past us and up the hill with some rather good speed to her. Over the hill she flies and out of sight.

The kids were still standing there in their moment of amazement. That look of disbelief of something they have not seen before. We move on down this path and the young mosses and lichens open up to the sun. The carpet moss was so furry for them to feel and see. They liken it to the carpet in houses.

We move on down and the young flowers are starting to open and feel this warmth of today. The touching they do to see why these flowers are so soft. This rather new experience for them is quite extensive. Taken all the words in and feeling all that I speak. Their minds whirling with excitement and joy at the opening of Mother Earth's heart.

To many Spring has arrived on some day in March but to us spring has arrived with the opening of Mother Earth's heart. She starts to bring forward her many ways of taking care of us. The four-leggeds moving around now for more food as the young grasses make their way towards the sun.

We find our place that we want to sit and I play my drum while the kids sit and listen to the beats echo throughout the land. I welcome the coming of spring and the warm winds and the life it brings upon the land. I pray and am thankful for the regeneration of Mother Earth on this land. Another year has been granted and we shall make full use of it.

As I finish my prayers and songs a beautiful friend appears as he glides on the wind so close to us. Our good friend the Cetan (hawk). He flies ever so quietly and calmly watching as I sit and pray. Making his circles that glide so easily.

The kids watch him with wondering eyes. They watch him make his circles above us. They watch with strong eyes that remember what I told them about him. They watch with honor and respect to him. A good friend indeed.

This day marks our first day of spring. For Mother Earth has shown her many gifts that she will bring forward for us. The Cetan has marked this day with us and honored us with his presence. Honored us with this wonder long waited for.

When Mother Earth Opens Her Heart.

The Tree And The Flower

◆

One day there was a tree and a flower that sat close to each other on a large prairie. The sun was shining bright and the air was crisp with the warm summer breeze. The grass flowed freely and bent with the wind. The flower sitting there with its green leaves and brightly colored flower blazing its scent and color across the prairie for anyone to see and smell.

The tree stood there wide and tall with its branches flowing outward. Its branches floating freely on the gentle breezes of the wind. The branches were full of bright green leaves that glistened in the sun. The tree was majestic but very much humble to what it has become.

One day the flower had many visitors to its pedals, which made it glad. The flower was proud that it was noticed and liked among the insects that visited it. The flower boldly spoke and said with such fact, "I am well noticed for I can spew my scent out to those that want to smell and follow it. I am feeling good about myself for I have brought these things to me and they have pollinated my flower."

The tree looking down in a rather disappointed sort of way spoke his words quietly and softly, "Your flower is bright this I must truly say, but your words are too strong for you notice little of why they have come to this land. They come not for the brightness of your flower or scent but for the food that is all around you in this wide-open land. Your words are arrogant considering how small you really are. They come to me as well to feed on these flowers that I bear. They feast in the powder that collects within all flowers. No matter who they are or where they stand."

The flower shot back, "but you just don't get it do you? I am very bright and I am for a reason. I am better than you and this I can prove. I am well known throughout these parts that spread so far and so wide. The truth that I speak will stand long before my eyes."

The tree just sat there in nothing but amazement, for the flower refused to see what was truly being said. The flower sat there so smug in its glory and gleam. It was proud that it had proven that a flower is much greater than a tree. It refused to see that that tree was covering its head from the storms that came by. Covering its head from the rains that devoured all else in its way.

The tree just stood there doing just what it does best. Sheltering all that need its protection. Giving life to those that know where to look and using its branches to support all life there.

Later that day a four-legged came walking along. It smelled the rich scent of that wonderful flower. Its rather strong scent was sweet to its nose. It wanted to find from where this scent flowed. And see where it grows. It came on the flower and there it sat in its glory. Sitting there so brightly and smelling its own glory.

The four-legged smelled that flower like no other it did before. It seemed there was nothing like it that met its grand smell. The four-legged was so impressed it just couldn't wait. It opened its mouth and ate that flower head. The tree sat there in horror at what it just saw. That poor flower had lost its lovely smell and its bright grandeur.

The moral of this story is nothing to seek.

When you open your mouth, you better be prepared. For what you seek may not be what you want. The power of words flows strong and flows true. The power of words may one day come back to eat you.

Knowing Where The Path Walks

◆

Teaching survival skills must open as many sides as possible for them to understand where a direction lies. Today was a good day to think and teach about the future. It was a day to help the kids think about both the good and not so good ways to walk. Good and not so good from many sides, not just one. To be able to look at something or somewhere and "know" fairly close what was going to happen and approximately when.

The day was cloudy and the drizzle laid its fine mist over these lands. A blanket of opaque film that almost seemed to be, like a curtain. There were words spoken of the need to always keep an eye on the future while keeping the ear to the past. Both of them together making the present where the gate tends to open one way or the other. The future can never be made until you speak to the present for it must pass through to get to the past. Standing within a place never guarantees your future. The Creator never guarantees anything for anyone. Many feel as though they "know" where their destiny lies but this is just a fleeting thought within a moment. There is never any substance to these thoughts for they lie to far away for an accurate perception. Most times it is just a "hope" that they are going to get there. Never thinking that many paths exist within one.

We sit here watching the clouds loom off in the distance. They move across the sky like a leaf flowing with a stream to some unknown destination. The sunset is gleaming with colors of the rainbow over the grasses newly growing in this season. The flowers growing all over the forests and fields with their bright colors gleaming in the sunset.

Explaining how someone must look at each step and their consequences on each to determine which way might be the best. With each step your survival is determined. With each thought the path turns one way or the other. Both moving at the same time but independent of each other.

Watching the Plant Oyates grow helps them to understand the succession of lives within a circle. Circles are within circles and all are moving within the path. All of them moving down the path towards some known unknown moment. All known and unknown at the same time.

The animals are good for them to watch for they learn things that humans aren't able to teach well or as easily. The Plant Oyates live their cycle of life with each turn of the circle, with each completion of the seasons. The Sun walking its journey across the sky to rest once again for the night. The clouds acting like a blanket to keep it warm.

They speak words of wonder as to what happens when stone rolls down the hill. Wondering if they will be like it. Making a smooth way down to the bottom before the final resting place or hitting everything in sight before resting. Wondering if they will grow in their knowledge so they don't hit all those bumps, trees and so many other things before they come to rest.

The future depends so much on our perception of the here and now. Being able to "see" what and where the future lies. How can someone know if they will be here tomorrow or the next day? If you have learned to walk with an open heart and mind the future will never seem so far off. The unity of both can always foresee things about to happen. The balance of both never lets anyone down.

The future is as close as putting one foot in front of the other, one thought after the other. The key is to know where that path walks and where those thoughts lead.

Walking with Courage takes Endurance

———— ◆ ————

Today I took a walk into the world of the past. I wanted to see what the limits of my courage might be. The limits of courage I personally wanted to see and feel. Many speak of this in many ways but few know the "true" limits of what one can see or feel. Feel and know the limits of one's endurance. The courage to endure things emotionally, physically, mentally and spiritually.

To be able to walk in any direction takes courage. Walking the trail of endurance takes much courage. As I walk this path I have taken before, you see and fee many of the same sights, smells and fears that once were and still are.

Very few know what the Old Ones and Ancestors saw or felt in their day. Walking anywhere was a challenge and took a lot of courage to do so. Everyday was a challenge depending on what happened, or did not happen.

Courage leads to endurance and endurance leads to courage.

Walking the talk takes a lot of endurance much in the same way it takes courage to deal with the endurance of the talk.

As a Winged One seeks endurance to raise its young no matter what tomorrow brings, it also has the courage to continue on. It continues to see the courage in order to deal with the endurance to go on. Not give up when things get tight. The courage to go through and endure the storms and other bad weather for it sees that it will make it to the good days.

Raising children takes courage. You learn to endure. You pave the way for courage. Courage allows us to endure things we otherwise would not. The children watch and see what we do. They will know when they come into this that they will know what to do so that their endurance would one day be lengthened by our courage today.

Building on the endurance of today brings courage not only for us but also for our children, their children's children and on down the line. One step always builds on another. It just depends on which direction your walking in those steps.

The Old Ones walked on the courage of their past. The courage of today will help our young ones to walk their path to endurance. Building on their courage day by day so that they may endure what or if anything comes their way. The courage of today helps to build the endurance of tomorrow.

Walking the Road Back

◆

Today was a day where things seemed to move in all directions. Nothing was specific but all seemed to move in a direction it was supposed to. Walking the road back is not easy as one thinks. Some seem to think psychics really see the past. This is true only to a point. Within that point there are many variations of that truth. All off it is related to the perceptions one has when looking at an incident.

As you walk you come upon many things that allow the perception to get clouded. Your walking and something comes out of nowhere and blocks your path. You lay road markers along the way and many times watch for landscape makers that will allow better access and comfort when walking regularly along this road.

At times things can get dicey and precarious but you watch for these the next time through. This is an easy way but a very difficult one at times also. Images can move and twist in ways not known. They can be seen from different directions but with different perceptions all together.

Spirits just don't lie there and let everyone walk all over them. They move about like you and I. The Spirits move easier there than we ever could here. There are many things that are only hidden when the perception has not been reached or changed in a way to allow it to be seen. They walk this road frequently and at times stop to say hi or move right on by.

Walking the road back takes a lot of energy, time and patience so that what needs to be seen is seen with the eyes that it should be seen with. Emotions can flare up when seeing things back there and they too must be held steady or you will no longer walk that path. It will be much harder to walk the next time around. No guidance will you be given as you walk the road back.

Natives have known this way for so many seasons there is no way to count the length of time known. There are many that walk this road. They are familiar faces along the way. They are comforting to see and sit along side of when time is taken to speak of the ways. They speak of many ways that were once known among our People but now are lost.

They reminisce about things of Old and how things used to be and how they once were a proud people with little cares except what was pressing at the moment. Life was enjoyed as much as possible because you were not sure how long you were allowed to be on Mother Earth. Many are young and quite spry while others are far up in age and wisdom.

Some are in every age as there are in people. Pretty much like here on Mother Earth. There is much to see and hear about along the road. Many want to speak their tales and have you come and listen to the Old stories. They want you to come rest yourself with them a while and talk. Allowing you to see the sights in the area before you move on your way down the road.

The People are wonder to see and hear from. They are glad anyone who is able to stop by and speak the words with them. There are many things there also that many don't want seen either. There are many side roads that can lead you into areas not yet known. These areas are those places where murders and bad medicine resides.

In this place you must be careful for if you aren't careful there can be many things that will befall you there. Here is where many things are that try to remain hidden but eventually come out. Walking here can cause one to shudder with fear and apprehension. This place has a feeling of heaviness and the air is filled with a smell of something I cannot describe or bring into words.

Walking into this area can lead you far away from the place where you started.. It goes on for many moons and seasons. Here is where you must walk when trying to find out something about someone or incident that happened. Here you can find it.

The past is filled with areas that many don't want to see. In the future this will change. People will want to know what happened to the Ancestors and where they have gone. The truth of the past cannot be hidden for it comes out of the ground like grass out of the prairie. It sprouts like a flower and blooms for all to see. The Spirit World mimics Mother Earth. The only thing we have to do is look in the right place.

Within Life

———— ◆ ————

Tonight I sit here looking towards the Western sky with wonder on my mind. Wondering where the sails have turned the raft now. Within Life there are things we take for granted. When they are lost for a time we wish they were back with us. Not until we reach a point will that ever be.

Within the Heart, Life becomes itself. Within Life, the Heart learns to live.

Love falls somewhere in between so that we may live Life in a way that brings us what we want. Floating in our own canoe on the Seas of Life is both a wondrous and a dangerous endeavor.

Within Life, Love acts like a paddle to turns us in one direction or another. Turning us into the Wind or against it. Our boat moves within the waves produced by the Wind. Some are high and wide. Some are nothing at all. Other times the Seas are calm and navigable. When the Seas get rough we hope that Love will hold us together and not allow the canoe to fall apart.

Within Love there is Life and within the Heart the compass moves.

When we stand on our canoe and look around, we wish for things to be just as they are. Never Changing. Never moving so that we can repeat what we have enjoyed. Live what we always wanted to live. Breathe how we've always wanted to breathe.

Within Love there is Life and Within the Heart the compass moves.

When we stand on our canoe and look all around, we wish for things to be just as they are. Never Changing. Never moving so that we can repeat what we have enjoyed. Live what we always wanted to live. Breathe how we always wanted to breathe.

Within Life there is so much to navigate. The canoe sails on and the Heart guides as it will. Guides us to things we need to see and feel. Guides us to fee what we need to see. The Heart sees and feels before we want to realize what it is and where were trying to go.

The sails flow in the Great Spirit's Wind ever so quietly. Flapping away with all the confidence it needs for it hears the quiet whisper of the Great Spirit. There is nothing for these sails to fear for they are connected to it. Even on the calm days there is a breeze it feels and floats to.

So, if you see me I will be sailing by. Give me a wave for we are all Within Life. Within Life we will see the canoes of many of our People and Ancestors. Much we will be taught about the Heart and how it lives Within Life. The compass helps to turn the canoe through rough or calm waters.

Within Life, the Heart learns to live. Within the Heart, Life becomes itself. Within them both love embraces all.

Walking in the Lands of Another

◆

Today we went for a ride the North. We drove for a time while the Sun made its way across the path it must walk. The air was hot and dry. The grass was dry and crunchy. The trees sitting there hoping for the clouds to make their way from the West

And drop some moisture their way.

We drove our path towards the Lands of Another. These Lands I dreamed about. I did not know what to expect. Apprehension was there because of the exceptional heat that was occurring today. The open Prairie was no place to be in 102-degree weather.

Thoughts of what I would feel were on my mind. Many things could be there to see. Traveling to the North we moved ever so steadily. We started to reach the edge of the prairie as the Land opened itself right up before us. Open before us was the prairie Lands of the Pawnee.

Here there were past encampments of my Brothers and Sisters. These Lands traveled in all directions. These Lands opened like a book. When we reached our destination the Land was dry and a little dusty. A Cetan (hawk) pointed the way to the area where we were supposed to be.

The Land possessed the animals of the pronghorn, the coyote, the eagle, the prairie dog and many other animals. Winged Ones make their homes here. The Land, despite its dryness, was still teeming with life. The junipers were still green in their leaves. The dirt was ever so dusty and dry.

This reminded me of the roads that ran across the prairie so well known but where none can be seen. The roads of nowhere lead to somewhere despite their lack of clarity over the rolling plains of grass and sparse trees. The rez roads they are called but none can be seen.

A storm loomed off in the distance from us. I walked to the edge of the cliff to look over at the buttes in the distance. Their spires shooting toward the sky but yet still had a commanding presence to them. Their size stood to the test of time much like these Lands have.

The feelings of these Lands are something that must be felt. It was a feeling of a People that still are a commanding People. There have been many stories and things that I have heard. I wanted to experience it first hand myself. No opinions or blinders on. No words to block my mind and Heart from these Lands.

These Lands possessed a feeling of great pride. Feelings from a People that were much like my own. They loved to live and play. They loved to play games, tell stories and speak legends. Their knowledge had their own way of making a trail to someplace. Laughter still existed here much like it existed anywhere else.

As the Sun started to set the Nighthawks came out to float on the Wind from the storm in the distance. Their wings were floating quietly within the Wind. The hearts of many People have floated o their wings.

The Land stood quietly around these buttes there was. Life still lived regardless of who or what crossed these Lands. The Sun was setting on the other side and the colors of purple, oranges, reds, and yellow blazed their way across the Sky. Setting for another day so that it and this Land may rest.

It wants me to stay longer but I am unable to stay this day. I will one day again return to these Lands and find out what it wants to tell me. Speaking so quietly and ever so firm. I will return to it and stay for a while. I will sit beneath these majestic stands of rock. Listening to their wisdom. Listening to their songs. Listening to their pain as they have seen and felt for many moons and seasons.

I will walk on the Lands of Another so that I may see how my Brothers and Sisters walked their Way. Walked a proud way despite what I have heard. Walked a Path like all of us but no less nonetheless.

The Land speaks so many things to so many people. The Land talks of a People that lived good lives. Their thoughts, feelings and words still live here within and around these buttes.

There is a big difference in what people speak and what they know. Many speak they are one with the Land but are like a mix of oil and water. In order to become the Land the composition of the Spirit must change. In order to do this you must go and allow the Land to change you the way the "Land" wants you to change. Not the other way around.

The Land accepts those that are willing to change so that it meets with it and becomes a part of it. Not just sit there and contemplate their navels. The Land speaks much and listening is a big part of it. When the Land calls I go, for it is trying to tell me something. These Lands speak of a time when the People walked softly but walked a way of the Spirit much like our People have.

When the Land asks to speak I go no matter what I am doing. This at times irritates people for they are brought along on a moments notice. I always speak to them and say, "When the Wind blows does it give notice to those that I coming?" They go sometimes in reluctance but learn much while we are on the road and while we are there.

There is much to see and know while walking the Land. It speaks from our Ancestors and the Old Ones that have passed on. Their knowledge is still there. It is just that you must learn to know where to walk and where to listen.

The young ones must know where to go and where to walk. They must know where to see and listen so that the knowledge they want and seek can be found when we pass on our way. The knowledge is earned when the Land has learned to trust those that walk on her. She does not trust easily or quickly.

The Dilemma of
Animals and Their Trust

◆

The dilemma of animals and their trust is something that is hard to deal with. When taught to understand and learn from them they at the same time become a food supply. When trying to explain this to the young ones it is most difficult to show them both sides without the confusion it leaves behind.

The teachings and wisdom of the animals is priceless and cannot be ignored by them. As the path turns in different directions animals appear to show us different things and different ways of doing things. There is wonder as to what to do when eating is a problem.

The wisdom of the situation is different from the food supply it brings. When walking to learn what you want to do and need the wisdom of the animal this is different from going out and looking for something to eat. The only problem that could occur is that if the same animal appeared and you were looking for food and it

Was the only thing in sight.

It depends on the wisdom you listen to decide if it would be the one that is sacrificing itself for you. This in itself could be a lesson in regard to what position you stand to see the difference. Many animals and insects have crossed my path and they have imparted many things that are quite helpful in daily routines ands situations.

Lately trust of the animals has been a good thing but leaves me with the wonder if a situation might occur someday that it may be a choice as to what to do in this situation. It is like having a pet for a long time and having its trust and then one having to eat them.

The same people interpret many different things many different ways. A balance must remain at all times when dealing with this situation. A decision of who lives and who passes on is a decision that one-day may occur. Trust is a highly prized agreement between anyone and the animals.

They will feel and know the difference in this situation. They will wonder if in fact you do. If you will know what will happen when this situation arises. To a hunter there may not be any problems. But to someone who has gained the trust of the animals this may not be so cut and dried.

Learning the difference between the two will take some time. Learning the balance will take even longer. It will be well worth the walk.

Walking Within The Sacred Circle

———————— ◆ ————————

Not long ago I took a ride. I went for a long walk within the Sacred Circle that was spoken about by Grandfather. This Circle walks for many, many miles and encompasses many Lands. It travels in all directions. It covers many things and Peoples. The Circle still exists around our Land, the Land we call "Paha Sapa," the Black Hills.

As I traveled to the Land of my People, the Circle opened itself up to this travel. On the road to the Paha Sapa there were many things that happened. From the "shadows" walking along the prairie, to the Cetans (hawks) and the Wanblis (eagles) that traveled in front and along side of us.

Many pay no attention to what travels with them when they walk, ride or fly anywhere. The Spirits listen to our every word that we speak, be it good or bad. They wait to see if we need their help. We only get this help when we are sincere in what we want and say. Without this they cannot help for it may turn the Circle in the wrong direction or cause you to walk down the wrong road.

We traveled North for some time. The day was hot and dry. The air was filled with dust at times that seemed to choke you at a moments notice. The animals could be seen eating and drinking as if oblivious to this kind of heat. The Land quietly moved by as we traveled up to this hot, dry and dusty road.

Later in the day we finally started to enter Paha Sapa. Here we started into the Lands of my People. The trees appeared dark as the story of why we settled in these Lands. When you look from a distance you see the Paha Sapa and they appear black. I think this is a combination of the color of the trees, Ponderosa pine I believe, and the bark that has streaks of black that run down their trunks.

As we drove into Paha Sapa there we saw an increase in the number of animals that were around. There was one thing that I was nervous about. In the distance there was a fire, or rather a couple of fires that had started by way of lightning. They had tried to put them out but they were unable to contain it as well as they wanted.

The smoke rose high above the Paha Sapa to cover the Sun in a yellowish glow or hue. This is not a good sign for it meant that not only were the woods burning but the possibility of the fire taking the lives of so many of our brothers and sisters of the Plant and Animal Oyates.

I turned in the direction of the East and moved my way around this. It saddens me to see such things but this is the way of Mother Earth. She produces both good and bad on both sides of the path. She does what she has to in order to create a balance within her. This is a necessary step I try hard to let sink in.

The Paha Sapa are a Land full of life and sounds, Just that at times it may not be the life and sounds we want to hear.

As you travel these hills you see many tall trees and rolling plains at times. The "hills" at times get high and a cliff here or there jumps out at you. There is an opening that allows you to enter the Circle that is close to Paha Sapa. Paha Sapa is a very important part of our culture and our lives.

As I got around the fires we headed back North again to regain our original path that I had wanted to take. We traveled only for a short time for the Sun was making its way down over the mountains where it was time to rest. We found a place that was cheap for us to stay at and we slept in the ol' Native style, 3-4 people to a bed.

One thing I had noticed as I drove into this place is that the "air" of feeling was quite different than other places before. It appeared to become more pronounced than before. This I didn't know why at the time and needed more to "see" before I make any rash decisions.

We stayed at a motel that was the cheapest there was at this time of year. The lady there was nice to the ones in front of me but when she got to me she asked too many questions and asked for identification when none was asked of anyone else. I was even paying cash, no credit card or whatever to worry about.

Her rather "obvious" attitude was so close to racism it reeked of it. I couldn't allow this form of stupidity to continue. I spoke up a bit and she stepped back a bit and she spoke quickly of what needed to be done and the "rules" that had to be "obeyed." I only smiled under my breath and left.

The kids were finally settled in and ready to sleep. I could not due to the many things that were on my mind. I went outside to sit on the park bench that sat there. Out on the road the police drove up and down at least four times and I wondered as to the reason for this. Was this the only street that this particular policeman drove on? What was his purpose on this short stretch of road? Who or what was he looking at over here? All I could do was wonder.

Tonight I sit here facing the South thinking of the visions I have had today. Thinking about the woman at the front desk who face and attitude changed because I was Native. She, who appeared to be the proprietor of this establishment, treated me like she was afraid of me. She acted like I was unwanted or inferior in some way.

It is sad that every time I come to visit I get some sort of unwelcome attitude or remarks of some kind. It seems that my money is not good enough in some way.

I am sitting here thinking about the visions I have had since coming on this journey, I had another vision just a moment ago of being here before when In fact I have not been. Just before this I saw shadows on the Land at the beginning of the Paha Sapa.

I am feeling the fear and the jealousy of the White People here. The sky is clear and the cool wind is blowing from the South. The Ponderosa pines on the way showed their usual color, that for they were named for, Paha Sapa.

I am looking forward to this trip but at the same time a little apprehensive due to the multiple feelings and visions I am having. I brought my Buffalo drum and blanket for drumming to the Ancestors and my People.

The Moon in its light shined on my left, which lit up the few clouds in the sky. They floated by among the twinkling stars all around. The six foot high fence makes me wonder who or what they are trying to keep, or in for that matter.

There is much here that is unseen. There is much here that can be cut with a knife without difficulty. It continues to pile on like there is nothing there. Nothing for them to care for or care about in this Land. Non-trust seems to be the way of life here.

Walking an Unknown Road into Tomorrow

◆

Today a long and much needed walk was taken. Not only by me but the kids also. A walk that was both enjoyable but at the same time was laid with questions that only the future will answer. We walked the dusty road down to the bottom and watched the animals in their worlds. Living as if nothing had happened around them. They watched us with a curiosity that even I found leaving me with questions within my own mind about their looks.

We for the first time here in this land we were allowed to see a young porcupine. It was not a good situation though for the neighbor's dog. She was curious like all young ones are. When snooping to see whom this other young one was it laid its tail into her face. Quills impaled themselves into her chin, nose and paw. This was not a good thing because they will infect themselves quickly if left for too long.

The neighbor left her youngest with us while the veterinarian came from a long distance to meet her in the next town. She left in a hurry and we stood there watching her fly down the road in a cloud of dust. A lot has happened around these lands in the past few weeks. The young ones do not understand all that is going on. Their minds become confused at the adult's constant fixation on the TV, the radio and newspapers.

When trying to explain what is happening to these lands and how everyone reacts differently becomes a chore at times. The F-15 fighter jets that have flown in this area for a little while has them asking why are they doing what they are doing. "Why are they circling around our house like that?" one would ask as they run from side to side of the house as they circle the area.

The loud noise of the afterburners would make the ground and house shake in a way I found quite annoying. I stand there wondering how these fighter jets can protect these young minds. Wondering how can all this machinery protect that which is unseen, unknown and cannot be measured in any way. These machines give a sense of ease just in their presence. But what about all the other ways?

The young ones hear on the TV about all the abuse and discrimination from people, companies, the government and all the other things that make them wonder what is happening to their world. People say they should be sheltered from these sorts of things. This would be a mistake for they would not understand how to deal with these types of situations. They would not learn how to deal with these things and not fly off the handle in a heartbeat.

We walk watching the Cetans (hawks) playing on the Wind. Their carefree style of flying is good to see. Like there was not a care in the world. Questions arise about why the buildings fell on the East Coast. Why did those people fly them planes into those buildings? Where did all those people go when the buildings fell? Will we all die like that someday? Why is there bad medicine in people? Do I have bad medicine? Do my friends have it?

Question after question regarding the events of the past couple of weeks came from their lips. Some of these questions are loaded depending on how they are perceived and answered. The young ones try to understand all that has happened and at times they just can't. They will not be able to until they have gotten a bit older and are better able to understand these events.

I remember a story about Spider and Rabbits.

One day Spider (Iktomi) was walking along the prairie. He was growing more and more hungry as the sun walked its path across the sky. As he walked he came across a single tree that was there. He was growing hot and tired. He felt he could gain some rest before moving on. He could also climb the tree and see if he could see anything. As he sat near the top he spotted some Rabbits (Mastincala) off in the distance. He could not ignore this chance to play his tricks and fill his belly. His pouch was always filled with these tricks.

He climbed down and started to walk towards the Rabbits. While he was walking he was trying to think how he could trick them. Trying to figure a way to play his devious tricks. He looked into his pouch to see what the Rabbits would want that he had. Rabbits saw him coming. They waited to see what he wanted. Iktomi arrived and sat down. He spoke. "I have traveled a distance. I am hot, tired and hungry. May I sit here for a time?"

Rabbits said, "No, come sit with us."

Spider looked into his pouch as if to look for some food he had there. Rabbits just watched. They sat there wondering what was in his pouch. Rabbits sat there while Spider rustled in his pouch. Rabbits finally asked, "What do you have in that pouch you are carrying?"

Spider said, "Just some tender young flowers I gathered on the way."

Rabbits loved young tender flowers for they were the sweetest tasting of all. When the air warmed after the snow they knew the young tender plants would sprout and they could have a feast from the long cold winter. These thoughts flew around in their minds. There weren't that many anymore so they knew the change of seasons was coming. Soon there would be no more of these until the air warmed again and made the snow go away.

Spider saw this and said, "Close your eyes and I will give you all that I have. I have more than my share to eat. We will have a feast."

Spider knew the only feast there would be was Rabbit.

The Rabbits closed their eyes one by one until they were all closed. They sat there waiting for Spider to set up the meal so they would feast on what he gathered. Then Spider pulled a club out and started to beat the Rabbits to death. They opened their eyes and yelled, "Run, run.

Spider is trying to wipe us out!" The ones that survived ran as fast as they could. Ran as far away as they could.

I explained to the young ones not to allow their eyes to close for this is when you will be taken advantage of. When you become complacent where you are there will always be something that will come along to change things for you. It could come in any form, from any direction. To live in fear is not only stupid but also worthless. You must use good judgment. You cannot allow yourselves to become so trusting of everyone. Another words, become simple minded. Once you have done this, you have done so at your own peril.

Where Does Strength Lie?

———————◆———————

Of late there have been many opinions regarding many things. Some of them are strong and good. Others are a bit weak. While others are somewhere in between. When you stand strong where does this strength come from? Physical? Emotional? Mental? Or maybe Spiritual?

The words that speak their meanings at times leave nothing there except puffs of smoke. They walk as if there is nothing there. Some have spoken with courage. But is this strength? Or just stupidity?

Is courage strength or is strength courageous?

I believe that neither is associated to either. I have known many who have strength but are as courageous as a worm. I have known some to have courage but lack the strength to hold it in their hand.

When you have the strength to hold that courage and the courage to maintain the strength then they become inseparable as long as the holder wishes it to be.

The "real" strength of a person comes from the times of hardship. Not the times of plenty and want. This makes men, women and children weak in all aspects. The have not honed their tools of strength and courage so that when times got hard they were able to survive.

Useful dialogue is good as long as the integrity is held in place. Once you walk that Road of the Fools you lose your strength. Courage becomes like a rainstorm that erodes the wash when it rains too hard. All disappears done the river with very little left to hold onto.

In short, when you participate in the arena of the exchange of words you can participate in many good things. But the field is also riddled with mines. If you do not walk carefully, the place that you step next may send you someplace you care not want to be.

Battling does not produce strength not does it produce courage. The Creator does. The Creator didn't "create" any of this, we did. The Creator gave us things so that we may do well in our journeys. He gave us the responsibility to be the Guardians of our lands. To raise our children in a good way so that when we walk our last walk we can be proud. To be able to pass so that our children will walk their paths better than we have.

Have we done well?

I think each one of us knows this. Our talk reflects our walk.

The shallowness of the strength and courage I have seen on both sides bad. We need techno. crap to show how "strong" we are. The strengths of the People lie within everyone as a whole. Not in machinery. Everyone can bomb the hell out of everything.

There will be no more strength and courage afterwards than there was when you started.

A Slow Journey

---◆---

Today was a day in which walking on this dirt road was necessary. We walk many roads but never do we look down to see what we are walking on. We take for granted we are walking on something we have chosen.

As we walked down this road, with all the sounds of many sizes of feet, there was a crisp sound and feel to the road today. I have wondered for many seasons who or what has already walked this same road or path. Who is walking before me that I am unaware of?

The little ones pay only to the attention of where their feet fall, nothing else. Making sure they do not hit a stone, hole or ditch in the road. Their laughter is good to feel and hear on this fall day. The air speaks of coolness and snow soon to come and settle things down a bit.

The events of these past month or so has gotten people edgy, sensitive to obnoxious things, worried about the ridiculous and many other things.

I have thought about how the Old Ones would have had meetings to try to settle things. The grandmothers and mothers would be keeping the little and older ones doing things so that their minds would not be concentrating on the events currently going on. Everyone would be doing as they should to keep the People together.

There would be nervousness but not a fear many feel today. The support system would be in place to help all those that we could. The respect that is would be there regardless of the differences people have. Things would get done, as they should.

The councils would send out messengers to other Nations to see how and what could be done to guard against intrusions and to map out what could and should be done. The clans would be preparing for anything that might happen once the threat is uncovered and located.

The warriors were prepared and enabled to do, as they must. Protecting, helping and doing just about anything to make sure all things got done. Their markings, shields, face paints and many other things reflect this journey.

The journey of the People was a slow one but a sure one. No matter what was happening the journey remained the same, a slow sure one. The strength was there to keep all the People together and keep the eyes to the front.

There was always an uncertainty to the future but the strength of the People held that future within the People. The future is the same today. Regardless of what is seen, heard, felt or known the future will remain just as it is, a slow journey. The future is still there. The only thing we have to do is walk one step at a time.

The Lands help to speak what the future holds and we as a People can hear it just as the Elders, Old Ones and Ancestors have.

Regardless of what we think we see the Sun will still walk it's road much the same way we walk ours, one step at a time.

Road of the Dead

◆

I am not sure who fits into any mold anyone projects in front of them. No one will ever fit into anything because each person is on his or her own path. No matter who it is. September 11th ushered in an era that may well be like no other.

Tell me why can't anyone walk forward?

Why sidestep?

Why backup?

Words mean little to nothing unless the walk accompanies this talk.

Who knows how to lead?

Why do people fear something that is no better or worse than anyone else?

The psychological game is a dangerous one. So why walk within it? Why play? A lot of smoke and mirrors there. a game that can haunt as well as steal your life away.

A life for a life. An archaic way to think. Barbaric even.

I think I will continue to walk this dirt road to somewhere. Look to see when the last one falls if it has all been worth it. The children will inherit the world that is being created.

Is this the world you would want to inherit?

Only fools walk the road of the dead.

Walking a Road into the Past

◆

Today I was walking along admiring the sunlight and listening to the breeze rustle within the branches of the trees and all around me. I listened to the words it spoke for there are many there. The sky is a beautiful blue with only a few whiffs of clouds making their way across to their journey at the end. I walk along here because the ancestors call again to see something that is needed. Here I walk thinking the same as the Ancestors have and many others as well.

I am walking this path so that I can walk the path of my brothers who were, and still are, being slaughtered by people who think they are getting away with things, more precisely, murder. They think that they are just some animals waiting for slaughter. They are mistaken, very much mistaken.

These people who are dads, brothers, and uncles, possibly even grandfathers. They walk among their families without the slightest twitch of remorse for their actions. They walk with their heads high and proud of what they have done. They feel that they are "better" in some way. They feel that they have done a service for "whomever people" they have justified. Empowered the people a little more with the taking of a life. A very false sense of empowerment.

They boast of their "conquest" to themselves and possibly others within "their" group. To do so outside of this would bring about things that, in fact, do not "empower" the people. It would cause a rather different view to be taken on their "activities." These activities would then be downgraded to where they belong. Dishonoring the same people it was meant to empower.

Some killings are accidental and without malice. Most are intentional and perverted. Within their minds they justify what they have done for their viewpoint has become twisted in some way within the spirit. They believe "they" are correct in their thinking. They believe they are the ones to survive within the world and gain all there is to gain from it. How can one gain something when life has been taken? Taken without the premise of self-defense or for the necessity of food. Done in a dishonorable way.

Just as we walk forward, the path always walks backwards. As we take steps forward those steps are walked backward so that these senseless acts can be addressed and laid to rest. The Spirits of these people must be laid to rest and begin taking their walk to the West once and for all.

In order for justice to be served it must first be resurrected so that there is something to follow. Fighting for justice does little than keeping you running after it. Fighting with it and along side of it allows for better vision. It allows for the eyes to see where to walk and find the clues to the killing. Find what is necessary to bring "justice" up and to the forefront and allow the Spirit of that person to finally walk home. Take the final ride to the Lands of the Ancestors where family and friends wait.

The Cetans (hawks) fly on the Wind with a grace that is good to see and watch. A young porcupine left its mark on a neighbor's dog. Small quills lie there waiting to be carefully removed from its face. It is a belief that this one will learn to leave those alone that can cause harm. Learned quickly she did. Until you learn where you must walk to solve these things there will be hazards as there was with the porcupine.

Knowing Where The Path Walks

◆

Today was a good day to think and teach about the future. It was a day to help the kids think about both the good and not so good ways to walk. Good and not so good from many sides, not just one. To be able to look at something or somewhere and "know" fairly close what was going to happen and approximately when.

The day was cloudy and the drizzle laid its fine mist over these lands. It seemed like a blanket of opaque film that seemed like the curtain. There were words spoken of the need to always keep an eye on the future while keeping the ear to the past. The two together making the present where the gate tends to open one way or the other.

The future can never be made until you speak to the present for it must pass through to get to the past. Standing within a place never guarantees your future. The Creator never guarantees anything for anyone.

Many feel as though they "know" where their destiny lies but this is just a fleeting thought within a moment. There is never any substance to these thoughts for they lie to far away for an accurate perception. Most times it is just a "hope" that they are going to get there. Never thinking that many paths exist within one.

We sit here watching the clouds loom off in the distance. They move across the sky like a leaf flowing with a stream to some unknown destination. The sunset is gleaming with colors of the rainbow over the grasses newly growing in this season. The flowers growing all over the forests and fields with their bright colors gleaming in the sunset.

Explaining how someone must look at each step and their consequences on each to determine which way might be the best. With each step your survival is determined. With each thought the path turns one way or the other. Both moving at the same time but independent of each other.

Teaching survival skills must open as many sides as possible for them to understand where a direction lies.

Watching the Plant Oyates grow helps them to understand the succession of lives within a circle. Circles within circles within circles. All of them moving down someone's path towards some known unknown moment. All of them known and unknown at the same time.

The animals are good for them to watch for they learn things that humans are not able to teach well or as easily. The Plant Oyates live their cycle of life with each turn of the circle, with each completion of the seasons. The Sun is walking its journey across the sky to rest once again for the night. The clouds acting like a blanket to keep it warm.

They speak words of wondering what happens when a stone rolls down the hill. Wondering if they will be like it. Making a smooth way down to the bottom before the final resting place or hitting everything in sight before resting. Wondering if they will grow in their knowledge so they don't hit all those bumps, trees and so many other things before they come to rest.

The future depends so much on our perception of the here and now. Being able to "see" what and where the future lies. How can someone know if they will be alive tomorrow or the next day? If you have learned to walk with an open heart and mind the future will never seem so far off. The unity of both can always foresee things about to happen. The balance of both never lets anyone down.

The future is as close as putting one foot in front of the other, one thought after the other. The key is to know where that path walks.

Lacking Assimilation

—————————— ◆ ——————————

There are times that seeing the drunks of our People makes me angry and upset at their behavior. Why they chose this way to walk. The lack of strength where strength at one time sat and held strong. Their strength was like lightning within the thunderstorm as the Thunder Beings rode across the sky.

I listen to their words and wonder, which way they could have walked if they had only chosen the way others have. Listening to the echoes of times gone past that once were but now are gone. Listening to their ancestors speak even though they don't hear them. Listening to the familiar ring that is present in their voice.

Even in their drunken state they want to live as their ancestors did. They just lack the ability to walk back to find the road that takes them in that direction.

The ones that are "leading" the People do not have a clue as where to walk to find such a road. Many walk around lost in some dream world thinking they "know" but really know little of what they speak. Such great "leaders" they call themselves. Leading themselves around in some kind of fog and smoke. Blinded by their own ego that has filled them with false hopes and dreams.

I have thought for a while that when they got drunk they did so on their own desire and ground. Now I find this not to be so true in so many people. They seek it for relief only from the assimilation "dream" that people seem to be following without any desire to fight it. Relief from the pressure of being like "everyone else." Like the wasicun. More like the wasicus anymore.

Walking the road back is by far not easy for anyone no matter who or what has been done. Not admitting to things is within the face of the coward. The coward who refuses to fight assimilation. Soon lacks an identity because he has "filtered" into the background of the wasicun. He or she no longer stands out anywhere. Just a small dot in the background of nothing at all.

They once had an identity that was strong. They held themselves in high regard for all around them but in time they grew weary and tired. They took that side road that lead them down this path. Their strength grew weak and their feelings grew no more.

They finally hid within the free flowing feelings of the bottle. Only coming out long enough to find it again and move into the next one. Walking down that path away from the road they were once on. The road of a proud and a prosperous People. Now down the road of the drunk.

To those that think the drunks of our People are weak lack knowledge of any kind. They are still as strong as they were. Problem is there is no one that can walk them back to where they once were.

They fought that road to assimilation. Thing is no one noticed. They fought hard and long until they gave up. They most truly at times lack assimilation. Lack it very well regardless of how much they drink. How many others can say they lack assimilation?

Very few I am afraid. Then there are those that are just plain stuck. And there are those that no longer want to remain separate from the crowd. They just want to be just as they are, what ever that may be.

Drinking is no way to walk for you stop walking altogether.

But what weak person would have the strength to constantly drink and die such a horrible death?

Winged Ones

———————— ◆ ————————

Today is a good day for the Sun is shining good with strong rays of warmth. It is walking its path with a good strong heart today. No clouds can be seen in any direction.

The Winged Ones are floating on a gentle breeze. No presumptions there. Nothing but calmness despite the chaos ensuing in some of these directions in other Lands. They sit and speak to each other much like we do of things, just on different ideas and thoughts.

They speak of things that are important to them. They speak of food and where to find it, their nests and how they are, the feelings they are getting from the Wind and weather today. What it will mean to them and others in the near future. Some of it is just talk. Just normal talks like the humans do.

They are speaking of how they are feeling today. Exchanging thoughts on their world and how it is changing around them. It is quite interesting to watch and listen to.

A Rabbit slowly approaches from the West and eats the grass nearby. His coat is fluffier and a bit lighter to match the trees and grass around here. Closely he watches the Winged Ones fly around. Watching to make sure that one of them is not the Cetan – the Hawk.

The Winged Ones are a wonder to watch. They float on the Wind with little difficulty and glide there with perfect ease.

They live and sleep like we all do. They seek shelter like we do. They act and react a lot like we do. They are families just like all things on these Lands. They have personalities that vary like we as a People do. They are a sight to watch and chuckle at, at times.

The words spoken by the ones are good to hear. Their songs can bring happiness to the heart. They speak only what they see and feel. No pretences or lies here. They live simple lives. Many times without anyone knowing it. People destroy the Land they live on for their own glory and ego.

Without these Winged Ones we would have such a good world to live in. They keep the insects in check so that they do not over run our Lands. Each thing on our Land has a purpose and a place. We do as well. We are not the highest things on the evolutionary ladder. Far from it.

Walking among these spirits makes one feel good. They bring their playfulness and heart to the Land. Each one has a place whether they are mean or pleasant. Their eyes see things that help us to see our own Land around us. They bring a unique view that helps us to live among all the other creatures among us.

They will open their world to anyone willing to listen. They will tell their tales and speak their words of wisdom. They will sing their songs. All that is needed is a willingness to sit and listen.

As the Sun Walks

◆

Today I took the Little Ones on a walk as the Sun made its walk across the sky. Its view and warmth was well welcomed here. There have been much clouds here covering its rays that spread its warmth and light. It was good to see and feel despite all that has and will happen.

The Little Ones enjoyed this walk for on it they saw the leaves fall and the Four-leggeds and Winged Ones making preparations for the upcoming rest period. The snow will fly and many things on these Lands will begin their rest period before making their way to the new season. The Fall colors will soon turn to brown. Nothing but brown and some green from the evergreens here.

Ceremonies and preparing what is needed is getting done as has been for centuries before. The Sun walks it path no matter what lies before it. It sleeps and allows another day to come for its People on the Lands below.

Teaching the Little Ones what is needed for this season helps them to make things better for the cold months ahead. They asked many questions regarding the activities of the four-leggeds. Asking why they are now coming closer and more personal. I explained to them that this was something that was done when the Lands learned to accept those that lived on it.

The Lands and Four-leggeds are one just like the Plant Oyates and we are. We all bleed from the same wound. There is no separation of any kind. There are simple things between us, nothing more. It the two-leggeds that make things hard for everyone in the Circle.

The Circle turns much like this planet we live on does…continuously.

We petted the horses and fed them their usual share of carrots they eat ravagingly like they haven't eaten for weeks. They come now whenever we walk this dirt road. The smallest one has learned not to be afraid of the giant ones before him.

As the Sun walks its walk, it walks with a strength and light that lets anyone use it without asking for anything in return. It brightens our lives and makes us feel good.

The Little Ones walk with a strong walk today. A confident walk they have not had in a while. They are learning to live life just as it was regardless of the possible uncertainties in their lives ahead.

I am admiring this for they are learning the Ways of our People. The strength and wisdom of the Elders and Old Ones. The Sun shines brightly as the strength and wisdom does. They are helping to teach them the things that are necessary for survival.

The need to pay attention to personal things is just as important as taking care of the larger picture. Regardless of what we think and say we are held accountable for these words. Words that carry responsibility back to the one that spoke them. All that walks before you will one day meet you face to face.

Let us sit by the fire and tell good stories. Let us laugh as we once did. Let us smoke the pipe so that there is nothing between us. Let us put our words and deeds so that the Ones after us will speak good things and remember us as we should be…..A Proud and Strong People.

As the Sun walks so does the Wisdom and Strength of the People who have walked before us.

Another's Walk into Desperation

◆

Tonight I am walking within a brother's life. An Apache man's life that was both Proud and had desperation within it. He walked a road less traveled. A road that was dusty and old. A walk that would take him into areas he didn't want to walk.

The road less traveled is one that follows the heart and does not allow any deviation from it. It never allows you to walk anywhere else. He walked where he could, as best he could. He would teach all that he knew and the secrets that lie within his Stories to them.

On this dusty trail were many places where he would rest but nothing more. He saw many of the things that would befall his People and why. He would see Visions that he really, after a while, did not want to. He tried to get others to understand such a road but the chaos was within everyone. Even the young ones who at one time sat at his side.

He was out of place within the world he lived in. He was a dinosaur now even within his own People. He was walking where the Old Ones have walked and now no more. He carried with him many of the Old Ways. Once he was allowed to walk his own Path to the Ancestral Lands these Ways would be gone.

He knew the only way to go back was to go back to the Land and the Ways that it spoke and taught. He knew that the Ways he was taught would be gone once the last Sun set for him to the West. Loneliness filled his Heart as he walked this Path.

I sit here watching a man walk a Path that neither he nor his People wanted.

It was a path where he walked many places. He saw many things. This Apache man was gifted with a sight that would allow him to see what would befall his

People for years to come. It would end up that his People and many others would walk this road within desperation.

The pain that he and his People felt was within the Heart. When the Heart of the People lies dying then the Heart of the Land dies as well. As he walked and received his Visions he would wonder when these things would happen. His heart would sadden that he knew at some point they would occur and the People's existence would suffer.

The Path leads to nothing more than acts of desperation. Once the Old Ways would grow no more in the Sun he would pass on with a saddened heart. He would leave behind stories that would make people wonder as to what to expect but there was no consoling in them for no timeline was allowed. Nothing.

Only Visions lying in wait for their moment to occur. They would then step forward and make their gifts known. Only then would they see what needed to be seen and done. The dusty path leads to nowhere but yet it becomes something. The People still await his Visions to come and yet they do nothing to stop them. Only wait to fulfill them. Lying in wait as the Visions do.

The People still walk within the desperation. They think there is headway and that the Sun is rising in the East to greet them. Another Sun may pass its way to its place to sleep and the Seasons will walk their way past. The People cannot for they still search for their place to rest and sleep.

In Time

◆

This morning I sat here watching the winged ones landing on the grass and eating the seeds that were present there. They frolicked around flitting on the strong wind that was coming from the north. The clouds rolling quickly across the sky and clinging to the mountaintops like a blanket wrapped around their peaks.

The snow was starting to fall here for the air was chilling down as it usually did when a storm was ready to come through. The winged ones still eating for they have to keep warm in this, what seemed to be a regular pattern of up and down of temperature changes.

The changes that the land is undergoing are both minute and large. It is changing quickly and slowly at the same time.

I am sitting here watching the winged ones because they are our bothers and sisters. There are families, friends, sometimes fights between them over whose territory is what. Even though they know the snow is coming and will soon cover these seeds. They will always come back to this place for the seeds for it helps to sustain their lives and families.

The snow is falling at a larger pace as the clouds unload their weigh. The wind howls around these mountains like a wolf howling at the moon. The wind can be both friend and foe, It just depends on whether you have been accepted by it. The wind can carve things out of rock like a knife through butter. It can be gentle and whisper in your ear anything that you need to know.

Its fierce movement can teach just as much as its gentleness. The Winged Ones hang onto the ground with strength that at times is a wonder while the wind and snow blow fiercely around them. The Plant Nations are ever so silent in the cold of winter but still have a bit of life still present if you listen close enough.

The chirping of their conversations at times is hard to keep up with. They talk of things to come and their families. They talk of how fat one is getting without regards to the ability to fly, as sometimes it maybe needed. Their conversations vary depending on the mood they are in at the time.

The wings of these ones fly into the wind even though they know at times they will not get far due to the strength of wind. They manage to get to their destination regardless of flow. They persevere with a strength that I admire in these brothers and sisters.

The deer, foxes, raccoons and all the others are in their place right now because the snow is moving quickly across this land. There is life within the snow even when there is nothing around. A hawk yesterday rode the wind ever so carelessly looking for things to feed his family with. He moved quickly and silently on the wind. Up and down he sank with the currents that flowed through.

Many look at the hawk with a disdain I know little about. They don't like when they snatch food from them. Occasionally he snatches a cat that has wandered into a place that it shouldn't have. The cat looking ever so silently onto its prey while it itself is being preyed upon. Not looking and feeling in all directions before proceeding cautiously.

I have watched this circle of life on this land where such a variety of life sets itself. It is usually the stupid, young and foolish or inexperienced ones that die a young death. They do not look in all directions before moving. They take things for granted and "hope" that nothing will hurt them today.

The hunters that want that "prize" trophy and care little of the consequences of their actions. Killing of the Older Ones that can teach these young ones what to do and where to hide. Where is their "prize" when they kill of everything and leave nothing but young ones to fend for themselves.

People crucify Mother Earth when many die that shouldn't. How do you know this is not a balancing that goes on when someone kills something somewhere without a good reason for doing it?

In the future I think we will see more of this but with a slight twist to it. A twist that will lead to a greater "payment" for the stupidity that we are exhibiting now. In time we will see how we fair with our responsibility towards Mother Earth.

In time we will see if our children curse the ground we walked on or even remember our memory with a respectful way and for many generations to come.

Only in time will we see.

Sungmanitu Tanka (The Wolf)

◆

Sungmanitu Tanka is as far from savage and mean as the Sun is from Mother Earth. The wolf is a pathfinder. He finds his way, as he must. His sight looks far into things. He can hear and feel far into the day or night regardless of who or what stands near him. He is a hunter with keen hearing and sight. He hunts for his family and to maintain his way of life much like we as a People do.

We have Wolf Clans and Societies that mimic his behavior. Sungmanitu Tanka is a respected Brother of the Native People. His ways were learned by our People and followed because his ways were so close to our own. He was a strong Brother and an individual also. He had a keen sense of family much like we do. You were a person but still were a part of the People. Your opinion counted as much as the whole. Not squashed as quickly as possible.

Sungmanitu Tanka was good at patience and perseverance. He was able to walk quietly and steadily for what he was after. After a time he was able to hunt quickly and got what he was after most of the time. He sat quietly and listened for anything that seemed out of place.

He was a good teacher not only to his children but also to the rest of the family and clan he ran with. He would return to the pack, after a while on his own, to teach and relay what he had learned to the rest. He would also pass on his medicine for this is what he was known for. His eyes were sharp and pierced that which many would try to hide. His ears would perk up at the slightest difference in the Wind.

Sungmanitu Tanka's ways were copied for the Nation or Tribe resembled what he did. He would provide food for all much like the warriors and hunters did for the tribe. They saw to it that the children received their education so that they to would be proud and strong. The survival of the Nation depended on it. The warrior defended the territory that surrounded the Nation like the wolf did. The defense of the feeding grounds of the Four-leggeds was imperative for the long-term survival of the People.

The Wolf taught many things. He was noble until his death. He stood there and took what came even though he knew he was about to die. Some of the warriors even started to put their knives into the ground to say, "This is where I will die today. I will hold my ground until I can no more. It is a good day to die." Some others know this as the "Acknowledgment of Death." Within this moment there are words spoken between them. They know whether they will live or they will die. Within this moment there is a deafening silence before anyone moves. There is a proud moment. A noble moment indeed.

The Wolf is a Four-legged that is well respected and honored. He knew how to balance the Land around him. He never took more than he could use, or that of the pack. This way nothing was wasted. Nothing was left behind.

He taught and learned as much as he could for himself, family and pack. A proud hunter, protector and teacher. He has a strong sense of family. His medicine is strong. His words are true and sing on the Wind. His howls speak to all around him and speak who he is.

Sungmanitu Tanka. A True Brother indeed.

0-595-21019-8